Susan Downs

# Teaching Social Skills to Youth

D1532910

## Also from the Boys Town Press

The Well-Managed Classroom, 2nd Edition
Tools for Teaching Social Skills in School
More Tools for Teaching Social Skills in School
Show Me Your Mad Face
Great Days Ahead: Parenting Children Who Have ADHD with Hope and Confidence
Safe and Healthy Secondary Schools
Teaching Social Skills to Youth with Mental Health Disorders
Effective Study Strategies for Every Classroom
Tips and Tools for Implementing a Classroom Management System DVD
Working with Aggressive Youth
No Room for Bullies
No Room for Bullies: Lesson Plans for Grades 5-8
Competing with Character®
The 100-Yard Classroom
Changing Children's Behavior by Changing the People, Places, and Activities in Their Lives
Adolescence and Other Temporary Mental Disorders DVD
Raising Children without Losing Your Voice or Your Mind DVD
Common Sense Parenting® DVDs:
      Building Relationships
      Teaching Children Self-Control
      Correcting Misbehavior
      Preventing Problem Behavior
      Teaching Kids to Make Good Decisions
      Helping Kids Succeed in School
Common Sense Parenting®
Common Sense Parenting® of Toddlers and Preschoolers
Common Sense Parenting® Learn-at-Home DVD Kit
Time to Enrich Before and After School Activity Kit
Dealing with Your Kids' 7 Biggest Troubles
Good Night, Sweet Dreams, I Love You: Now Get into Bed and Go to Sleep
Parenting to Build Character in Your Teen
Practical Tools for Foster Parents
Skills for Families, Skills for Life, 2nd Edition

**For Adolescents**
Friend Me!
Guys, Let's Keep It Real!
Little Sisters, Listen Up!
Boundaries: A Guide for Teens
A Good Friend
Who's in the Mirror?
What's Right for Me?
Basic Social Skills for Youth

**For Children**
The Worst Day of My Life Ever!
I Just Don't Like the Sound of No!
Sorry, I Forgot to Ask!
Teamwork Isn't My Thing and I Don't Like to Share!
I Just Want to Do It My Way!
Making Friends Is an Art!
Cliques Just Don't Make Cents
Tease Monster
Getting Along with Others

For a Boys Town Press catalog, call **1-800-282-6657**
or visit our website: **BoysTownPress.org**

### Boys Town National Hotline®
## 1-800-448-3000
A crisis, resource and referral number for kids and parents

# Teaching Social Skills to Youth

**2nd Edition**

A Step-by-Step Guide to 182 Basic to Complex Skills
Plus Helpful Teaching Techniques

BY TOM DOWD, M.A. AND JEFF TIERNEY, M.ED.

BOYS TOWN Press

Boys Town, Nebraska

# Teaching Social Skills to Youth 2nd Edition

Published by Boys Town Press
Boys Town, NE 68010

Copyright © 2005 by Father Flanagan's Boys' Home

ISBN-13: 978-1-889322-69-8

All rights reserved.  Permission is granted to reproduce pages 61-257 for classroom or individual counseling use only. No other part of this book may be reproduced or transmitted in any form or by any means, electronic or mechanical, including photocopying, recording, or by any information storage and retrieval system, without the written permission of Boys Town Press, except where permitted by law.  For information, address Boys Town Press, 14100 Crawford St., Boys Town, NE 68010 or btpress@boystown.org.

Boys Town Press is the publishing division of Boys Town, a national organization serving children and families.

## Publisher's Cataloging in Publication

Dowd, Tom (Tom P.)

Teaching social skills to youth / Tom Dowd and Jeff Tierney. -- 2nd ed. -- Boys Town, NE : Boys Town Press, c2005.

p. ; cm.

Accompanied by a CD-ROM which enables searching the text using various approaches. Includes bibliographical references and index.
ISBN: 1-889322-69-5
ISBN-13: 978-1-889322-69-8

1. Social skills in children--Study and teaching. 2. Social interaction in children--Study and teaching. 3. Interpersonal relations in children--Study and teaching. 4. Socialization--Study and teaching. 5. Social learning--Study and teaching. I. Tierney, Jeff. II. Title.

HQ783 .D69 2005
303.3/2/07--dc22                    0508

15   14   13   12   11   10   9   8   7   6   5

# Acknowledgments

We would like to thank the following Boys Town staff members for their contributions to the revised edition of this book and for their commitment to providing a valuable resource for all those who strive to improve the lives of children: Doug Czyz, Kevin Lee, Jack Nelson, Debra Ondar, Clarence Reed, Kevin Murray, Barbara Lonnborg, and Terry Hyland.

# Table of Contents

**Introduction to Social Skills Teaching** ................................................... 1

Chapter 1
**An Overview of Social Skills Training** ................................................... 7

Chapter 2
**Elements of Social Behavior** ................................................... 11

Chapter 3
**Individual Teaching Techniques** ................................................... 17

Chapter 4
**Generalization of Social Skills** ................................................... 33

Chapter 5
**Teaching Skills in Group Settings** ................................................... 37

Chapter 6
**Social Skills and Treatment Planning** ................................................... 47

Chapter 7
**The Social Skills Curriculum** ................................................................. 55

Appendix A
**Social Skills Grouped by Skill Type** ...................................................... 261

Appendix B
**Social Skills Grouped by Character Trait** .............................................. 267

Appendix C
**Social Skills Grouped by Behavior Problem** .......................................... 277

Appendix D
**Social Skills Grouped by Situation** ...................................................... 293

**References** .......................................................................................... 301

**Bibliography** ...................................................................................... 305

**Index** ................................................................................................. 309

# Introduction to
# Social Skills Teaching

**B**efore he learned the skill of "Following Instructions," 10-year-old Damone would look down at the floor and mumble to himself whenever someone asked him to do something. If the person giving the instruction was lucky, Damone would carry out the task or activity, but his track record for following through was shaky. Even if he did the task, Damone didn't know that he was supposed to let the person know he was finished. He didn't have much confidence in himself because he just wasn't sure what was expected of him. People didn't have much confidence in Damone because they couldn't be sure he was reliable. At home and at school, Damone was often in trouble for not doing what he was told.

Damone's education in how to appropriately follow instructions started in school when his teacher began teaching students the skill as part of her class. Then she sent home some papers with the steps of the skill: Look at the person; Say "Okay"; Do what you've been asked right away; Check back. Damone's parents started working with him on learning the steps and practicing. Within a couple of weeks, Damone had the steps down, and his behavior began to change for the better. Now when someone gives him an instruction, he does what is asked quickly and with confidence. He gets along better with his parents and teacher, and they are proud of his progress. For this child, one simple, basic skill made a huge difference in his behavior, his personality, and the way he gets along with others.

Social skills like "Following Instructions" are nothing new – except to the children (and adults) who don't have them or know how to use them. The earlier children and adolescents (and even adults) learn and know how to use social skills, the more successful they can be.

Everyone needs social skills. Social skills are the tools that enable people to communicate, learn, ask questions, ask for help, get their needs met in appropriate ways, get along with others, make friends and develop healthy relationships, protect themselves, and generally be able to interact with anyone and everyone they meet in their journey through life.

Most importantly, these skills help youngsters begin to develop and build on the essential character traits of responsibility, trustworthiness, caring, respect, fairness, and citizenship. These traits provide young people and adults with the internal moral compass that enables them to distinguish right from wrong, understand why it is important to do what is right, and make good choices in their thinking and behavior. (The six traits have been identified as the Six Pillars of Character by the CHARACTER COUNTS! Coalition, a project of the nonprofit Joseph & Edna Josephson Institute of Ethics. [See the box on page 5.] The Coalition is a diverse partnership of

1

nearly 500 organizations that works to improve the character of America's young people by promoting consensus ethical values. Boys Town and the Coalition have worked together on youth-oriented projects.)

While the long-term goals of social skill instruction are generalization (using the right skill at the right time in the right situation) and internalization (making skills a natural part of one's everyday life), the short-term benefits to teaching children skills cannot be overstated. In fact, when children learn foundational skills like "Following Instructions," "Accepting 'No' for an Answer," and "Disagreeing Appropriately," it enables whoever is teaching to continue teaching and sets the stage for instruction in more advanced and complex skills. In other words, if a child knows how to appropriately follow instructions, he or she can be directed to adopt and use a variety of prosocial behaviors that make up other beneficial skills. It is the repertoire of skills a child develops over time that shapes how he or she functions in society.

A child who does not learn social skills and the basics of social interactions is at tremendous risk for failure in the classroom, juvenile delinquency, being ostracized by positive peers, or being adversely influenced by negative peers. Children who are never taught social skills develop their own habits and devices for getting their needs met, habits and devices that often conflict with what society views as acceptable behavior. The result can be an adolescent and adult life punctuated by violence, drug and alcohol abuse, failed relationships, incarceration, and the frustration of never realizing one's goals.

# Boys Town's Approach to Teaching Skills

Social skill instruction and achieving skill competency are so important to the success of young people and adults that they are an inte-

gral part of every child-care program Boys Town offers. Boys Town has been caring for children since 1917, and while times and children's problems have radically changed over the years, our approach of combining the "head" – child-care technology, research, and innovation – and the "heart" – compassion, caring, and loving guidance – has remained constant. All kids – especially those who are at risk or in danger of becoming at risk – need the kind of attention and help that brings about positive, lasting changes in their way of thinking, feeling, and behaving. Social skills hold the key to unlocking the potential for good that every child possesses.

Boys Town's mission is to change the way America cares for her children and families. Accomplishing that mission on a day-to-day basis is difficult, and requires commitment, sacrifice, and skilled caregivers. In addition to our long-range goals, Boys Town first provides a safe environment for young people where they can put their lives in order and, in many cases, begin healing wounds that run very deep. Within this caring atmosphere, individualized treatment focuses on enhancing a youth's strengths and improving his or her deficiencies.

At the famed Village of Boys Town near Omaha, Nebraska, and at nearly 20 other sites across the United States, the work that our founder, Father Edward Flanagan, began in 1917 continues today. Four major programs are responsible for the majority of direct and indirect care we offer. These programs are:

■ **Long-Term Residential Program**, where boys and girls live in separate group homes with trained married couples called Family-Teachers. In this family-style environment, each resident has his or her own individualized Treatment Plan to address behavior problems and is part of the larger community of youth. More than 100 group homes serve the needs of youth across the country.

- **Assessment and Short-Term Residential Program**, which includes emergency shelters and staff-secure detention facilities for youth who must be removed from a dangerous environment or who are awaiting a more permanent placement.

- **Ecological Family-Based Services Program**, where trained Consultants work with families who are in danger of having a child or children removed from the home. Treatment occurs in the home as the Consultant and family work together to enhance family members' existing strengths and develop new ones.

- **Ecological Treatment Foster Care Program**, which provides foster care for youth with more difficult behavior problems. Trained married couples (and sometimes trained single parents) provide a safe, loving environment as well as teaching and treatment for children for as long as necessary.

In all four programs, the source of all treatment is the Boys Town Teaching Model.

# The Boys Town Teaching Model

To understand the concept of helping children learn new skills and behaviors so that they can competently use them in society, one must first realize that we are in the "business" of bringing healing and hope to children and families. Everything we do is rooted in the human experience – the successes, the failures, the progress, the obstacles. Children are human beings, not products on an assembly line. Boys Town's caregivers are not robots programmed to perform the same task, the same way, every day. It is true that technology and theory (the head) are necessary, but so is genuine compassion and concern (the heart) and treating each youth as an individual with unique problems. Technology

without compassion is pure manipulation; love and compassion without good science is pure sentimentality.

While the Boys Town Teaching Model has its basis in learning theory, it has not adopted a "mechanistic" view of how a child learns, as have other models that take this approach. In the Boys Town Model, the child is an active participant in the teaching and learning that occurs. The child isn't merely told how to behave; he or she learns positive behaviors and how to choose to use them in many different situations. This "empowerment," or self-help, approach combines the active participation of the child with the active teaching of the parent or caretaker. The strength of this approach is that it teaches children prosocial skills and helps them build healthy relationships with others.

The goal of this approach is not to control children, but to help them take control of their own lives. This is an ongoing learning process. Boys Town's teaching methods utilize behavioral principles, while allowing children to integrate their thoughts and feelings into this learning process. And, unlike many other learning theory models, Boys Town effectively uses external reinforcement, where appropriate, to promote and maintain skill-learning and relationship development. This allows children to change intrinsically. Inadequate thought patterns change, negative feelings diminish, and inappropriate behaviors are replaced by positive behaviors for the youth and others.

In addition to teaching skills, other elements of the Boys Town Teaching Model include building healthy relationships, supporting moral and spiritual development, creating a positive, family-style environment, and promoting self government and self-determination. Together, these elements comprise a proven, research-based, outcomes-oriented, and effective approach to helping children. In our programs, we expect kids to get better, and they do.

While all of the elements of our Model share equal importance, teaching skills is what helps kids learn new ways of thinking, new ways of feeling good, and new ways of behaving. Through teaching, we give kids the skills they need in order to take control of their lives and be successful. Whether it's a parent who wants to teach his daughter the skill of problem-solving, or a staff member in a youth shelter trying to help a youth learn anger control strategies, teaching skills is the key to healthy child development and replacing problem behaviors with positive alternative behaviors.

## What This Manual Offers

This manual reflects and focuses on the importance of teaching social skills to youth of all ages, the elements of social behavior (task and behavior analysis), individual and group teaching techniques, generalization of skills, the role of skill-based treatment interventions for difficult youth problems, and the Boys Town Social Skills Curriculum itself.

Our Social Skills Curriculum of 182 skills defines the positive alternatives to many of the maladaptive and self-defeating behavior patterns in which a young person might engage. It is intended to serve as an effective resource and tool for anyone who works with children and adolescents. This includes teachers, staff members in long-term residential youth programs and youth shelters, foster parents, counselors, therapists, and others.

All 182 skills and their steps are presented in this manual (Chapter 7). Besides being task-analyzed into their specific behaviors, the skills also are paired with specific skill types – social, emotional management, academic, ethical/moral, and independent living – and character traits, and categorized according to behaviors and situations in which they can be used to address problems or enhance a youth's abilities. (See Appendices A, B, C, and D at the end of this book.) A compact disk at the end of the book contains these appendices and the entire Social Skills Curriculum. Individual skills and their steps can be printed from the CD.

**NOTE:** For ease of reading, we use the term "social skills" throughout this book when referring to all of the Curriculum skills in general. The specific skill types – social, emotional management, academic, ethical/moral, and independent living – are used to better define the link between individual skills and behavior areas. Definitions of the five skill types are on page 6.

Skills open the door to success for youth, no matter the setting in which they are taught. We hope these tools can contribute to and enhance your work as you bring about lasting change, instill hope, and prepare young people for the future that awaits them.

# The Six Pillars of Character

(As described by the CHARACTER COUNTS! Coalition)

## Trustworthiness

Be honest. Don't deceive, cheat, or steal. Be reliable – do what you say you'll do. Have the courage to do the right thing. Build a good reputation. Be loyal – stand by your family, friends, and country.

## Respect

Treat others with respect; follow the Golden Rule. Be tolerant of differences. Use good manners, not bad language. Be considerate of the feelings of others. Don't threaten, hit, or hurt anyone. Deal peacefully with anger, insults, and disagreements.

## Responsibility

Do what you are supposed to do. Persevere: keep on trying! Always do your best. Use self-control. Be self-disciplined. Think before you act – consider the consequences. Be accountable for your choices.

## Fairness

Play by the rules. Take turns and share. Be open-minded; listen to others. Don't take advantage of others. Don't blame others carelessly.

## Caring

Be kind. Be compassionate and show you care. Express gratitude. Forgive others. Help people in need.

## Citizenship

Do your share to make your school and community better. Cooperate. Stay informed; vote. Be a good neighbor. Obey laws and rules. Respect authority. Protect the environment.

*(In Appendix B at the end of this book, these character traits are paired with the specific Curriculum skills that can be used to teach and reinforce the traits.)*

# Skill Types

## Social Skills

Skills in this category are related to most situations in which a person interacts with another person or other people. These situations might range from having a private, one-on-one conversation with a friend, to asking directions from a stranger, to being with a small group of people in a doctor's waiting room, to being part of large crowd at a party. Social skills enable a person to appropriately communicate with, respond to, make a request from, and get along with other people.

## Emotional Management Skills

Emotional management skills enable a person to find and maintain a balance between not feeling anything and letting one's feelings control his or her behavior. These skills also help a person maintain self-control, stay calm in exciting, stressful, or frustrating situations, and make good choices under pressure. One major area where this is important is anger control. People who know which skills to use to prevent or control their anger and not become physically or verbally aggressive are able to stay out of trouble and solve problems or overcome obstacles in appropriate ways.

## Academic Skills

Completing homework and turning it in on time, studying, taking tests, reading, doing learning activities, and taking notes during lectures are just a few of the areas where having good academic skills is necessary. And while we usually associate academics only with school, these skills are useful in any learning situation, whether it is with a teacher in a classroom or reading a book or working on a computer to expand one's knowledge.

## Ethical/Moral Skills

Skills that help a person learn positive ethics and morals contribute to building character and developing a conscience. A person's ability to use ethical/moral skills provides the "moral compass" that helps him or her know right from wrong, good from bad, and prosocial from antisocial. Good character stems from knowing the right thing to do and following through.

## Independent-Living Skills

People are able to perform the activities of life – cooking, shopping, keeping up an apartment or house, managing finances, balancing a checkbook, looking for a job, buying a car and making payments, and many others – because they have learned how to take care of themselves. Independent-living skills prepare people to be on their own and to contribute to society as a wage earner, a good neighbor, a productive citizen, and an independent person.

*(In Appendix A at the end of this book, specific Curriculum skills are grouped according to these skill types.)*

# CHAPTER 1

# An Overview of Social Skills Training

Teaching social skills to youth is a daunting task that requires perseverance and dedication. It is a process that also calls for constant repetition and practice if caregivers are to make a critical impact on their youths' future development and overall social competence. Social competence, individual social behavior, and their outcomes require that youth learn social skills that can develop and improve their ability to communicate effectively, solve problems, maintain self-control, and enjoy self-efficacy.

This is a tall order because what has been taught and modeled for some youth is often inadequate and sometimes dysfunctional, creating serious development and life-event problems. This is especially true for youth who have contact with social services, the juvenile justice system, mental health services, and youth treatment programs.

## Social Skills Training and Social Competence

Social competence is the outcome of different behavioral, cognitive, and emotional components. Competence suggests that one has the ability to perform a given task or set of tasks in a way that is deemed acceptable by others. When looking at social skills and competence, we are interested in how a person is validated by his or her current social circle or environment. What makes social skills training challenging is understanding how the environment changes, and how the social validity of every social skill is dependent on the ability of youth to make necessary adjustments to the people and situations within that environment.

Defining the concept of social skills has been challenging ever since its inception. Depending on how a skill is viewed, most definitions focus on individual behavior and its effects and outcomes upon others. Gresham (1998) defined social skills as "socially acceptable learned behaviors enabling the individual to interact effectively with others and avoid or escape socially unacceptable behavior exhibited by others." Along with this definition, Gresham (1998) proposed a two-dimensional model of social skills and interfering problem behaviors in which social skills can be classified into three distinct classes: 1) social acquisition deficits; 2) social performance deficits; and 3) social fluency deficits.

Social acquisition deficits are defined as the absence of knowledge of how to execute particular social skills or a failure to discriminate when certain social behaviors are appropriate. Social performance deficits recognize the presence of a social skill or skills, but there is a failure to perform the acceptable behavior in specific situations. Social fluency deficits reflect the presence of a skill, but there is an inability to perform the skill because of a lack of appropriate models or practice, or inconsistent reinforcement when the skill is used.

These three classes enable us to assess youth behaviors and move toward determining an appropriate intervention. Also included in assessment is the determination of interfering problem behaviors, the second dimension of Gresham's two-dimensional model. Many times, youth have internalized or externalized problems, which compete or interfere with skill acquisition, performance, or fluency. This makes it necessary for recognition and intervention to occur simultaneously. Internal problem behaviors can be characterized as fear, social withdrawal, depression, etc. External problem behaviors can be characterized as impulsivity, aggression, hyperactivity, etc. (Gresham, 1998).

Social competence is a judgment made by others that reflects one's ability to perform a social skill adequately and receive appropriate reinforcement. If we are to effectively teach youth appropriate alternative or replacement behaviors that ensure that they receive ongoing reinforcement for recognizing, choosing, and using the right social skill, we must be able to identify and recognize factors that influence youths' performance of skills and allow them to be perceived as socially competent (Spence, 2003). These factors include the ability to:

- use interpersonal problem-solving skills.

- perceive and process social information.

- understand and choose the appropriate skill.

- manage emotions and affect while interacting with others.

- self-monitor and make adjustments to behavior as needed.

- understand and interpret any environmental contingencies that require the modification or adaptation of a skill.

These factors occur simultaneously and rapidly during any given interaction with others and are more reflexive than planned. Any part of an interaction that is planned reflects on a youth's ability to spontaneously solve problems and implement solutions immediately when appropriate reinforcement for the interaction is not obtained. This reflects the adjustments necessary during a sustained ongoing socially competent interaction. Addressing any competent social interaction requires knowledge, mastery, and fluency to be successful. Without these there will be misperception, misinterpretation, and possibly an escalation in negative behavior.

The philosophy of social skill instruction within Boys Town programs is that youth have strengths and weaknesses (identified problem behaviors), and that active, direct instruction and practice is a key to remediation and growth. Focusing on a youth's strengths provides a foundation and a starting place for building skills and alleviating weaknesses, and provides a positive approach to remediation and treatment. Positive, prosocial behaviors, including those that require growth, can be modeled, taught, and rewarded, and therefore, become viable alternatives for a youth who has gotten into trouble in such situations in the past.

# Benefits of Social Skills Training

Social skills training has numerous benefits and ultimately can assist in developing social competence. Benefits include improving one's ability to get along with others, maintaining self-control, regulating affect, increasing academic success, and improving self-esteem, self-confidence, and self-efficacy. As noted earlier, interfering problem behaviors can hinder or block a youth's ability to achieve social competence. Numerous studies related to specific problem behaviors and the use of social skills training to address them indicate promise in helping youth improve or develop increased social competence. Areas where improvements have been noted include aggression, juvenile delinquency, child abuse and neglect, and mental health disorders.

Another distinct advantage of social skills training is that it can be used as a primary, secondary, or tertiary intervention (Walker, Ramsey, & Gresham, 2004). As we will discuss in later chapters, varying interventions enables caregivers to do group and individual teaching and allows for general-to-specific intervention, based on the severity of the problem at hand.

Primary interventions are those that deal with teaching general social skills to larger groups of youth and do not target a specific skill for change. This intervention is focused more on developing and improving the overall positive climate of a program or classroom. A secondary intervention is more specific in its overall goal of dealing with youth who are having difficulties with a specific class or set of skills (e.g., self-control, problem-solving, etc.), and could benefit from focused social skills training. Many times, this intervention is done in small, homogenous groups, which creates more efficient and cost-effective teaching settings. Finally, tertiary interventions are focused on reducing negative, antisocial behavior that causes youth to be at risk for more restrictive interventions (e.g., foster care placement, incarceration, etc.). This intervention requires more intensive individual services and generally requires specific treatment designs that focus on greatly reducing or eliminating antisocial behavior that, if left unchecked, will likely result in major life problems as a youth gets older.

## Summary

Deficits in social functioning appear to be implicated in numerous behavioral problem areas that children, adolescents, and young adults face. While children of all ages can experience these deficits, developing the ability to interact effectively with others may be especially critical during adolescence. This is normally a time when a youth should be refining a variety of basic social behaviors and learning more complex skills necessary for the transition to adulthood (LeCroy, 1983). Youth need to become increasingly skilled as they face the developmental tasks of adolescence, such as identity and value formation, independence from family, and appropriate group affiliation. Without a strong social and psychological base from which to develop, many adolescents fail to negotiate these tasks successfully.

Social skills training programs have repeatedly demonstrated their effectiveness in developing a wide range of interpersonal behaviors and skills in diverse populations of children and adolescents (Kazdin, 1985). The quality of any social skills training effort is enhanced by understanding and recognizing the complexity of social interactions, choosing appropriate social skills for normalizing those interactions, and teaching them in meaningful ways that can be valued by the youth, their peers, adults, and society in general. Caregivers can use group and individual interventions that are designed and structured to enhance interactions with their youth to build important life skills and treat behavioral deficits on a daily basis.

# CHAPTER 2
# Elements of Social Behavior

The goals of a social skills training program for youth are to establish new sets of responses to social situations and to teach youth how to integrate their behavior with others in the environment. In order to accomplish this, caregivers working with the youth must have a clear conception of what constitutes social behavior and social skills, as well as a method of analyzing youths' current level of functioning. This chapter will focus on the functional relationships between a youth's behavior and the environment, the structure of appropriate social skills and task analysis, and methods of assessing skill deficits and targeting alternative responses.

## Functional Relationships of Behavior

A behavioral approach to social skills training first recognizes that all behaviors occur within a context of environmental events. A youth engages in a particular behavior or activity in a given situation in order to have some effect on his or her surroundings. Examples of this may include getting someone's attention, obtaining a possession, or being left alone. But the result of that behavior, whatever the original intent, also will have an effect on the youth. Thus, the relationship between a youth's behavior and the environment is bi-directional, or functional. The youth is affecting the social environment, while the environment is simultaneously affecting the youth.

The events in the environment that may serve to modify or control a youth's responses are numerous, but can be generalized into two main categories: antecedent events and consequent events. Both of these are closely associated in time with the occurrence of a behavior.

## Antecedent Events

An antecedent event represents the situation or conditions that immediately precede a behavior or performance of a skill. Often, the antecedent event is a cue to a person that a particular behavior would be appropriate in that situation. For example, a ringing doorbell is a cue, or antecedent event, for going to the door and answering it.

Antecedent events are critical when attempting to analyze a problem behavior a youth is using. A caregiver (parent, youth-care worker, teacher, or counselor) may be able to examine the events that immediately precede a negative behavior such as a tantrum or becoming physically aggressive, and begin to detect patterns in the behavior's occurrence. For example, a youth may begin to argue and whine when told "No," but not when he is asked to complete a chore. In this case, the antecedent event would indicate to the caregiver that more time should be spent teaching the youth the social skill of "Accepting 'No' for an Answer" and not as much time needs to be spent on teaching the skill of "Following Instructions." The pattern of antecedent events that may be observed around any particular behavior problem or skill deficit of a youth will help determine the appropriate alternative skill to teach.

It also should be mentioned that improvement in problem behaviors, as well as gains in social skills, can be accomplished through manipulation of antecedent events (Gresham, 1981). If a parent complains that his son always loses his temper when told to go to bed, observation may reveal that the parent walks into the living room in the middle of a television show each night and commands the child to go to bed. Changing the antecedent event by having the parent prompt the child 15 minutes before bedtime that bedtime is approaching and negotiating a bedtime that is after the youth's television show may be enough to prevent the problem from occurring.

Recognizing antecedent events and choosing correct responses can be a major challenge for youth with social skill deficiencies. Situations that are ambiguous, including ones where others give vague verbal or nonverbal responses, can be easily distorted and misinterpreted by these youth. Confusion over intent in ambiguous situations has been viewed as a major precursor to aggressive acting out in some youth (Patterson, 1982; Dodge, Price, Bachorowskie, & Newman, 1990). Therefore, one area of teaching that should not be ignored by caregivers who are attempting to improve their youths' social competency is the recognition of situational cues, and strategies for dealing with these cues when they can be confusing or easily misinterpreted.

# Consequent Events

Consequent events (or consequences) are the outcomes that result after a particular behavior or skill has occurred. Broadly speaking, behavioral consequences can be classified into two general types: reinforcing and punishing. Reinforcing consequences invariably strengthen the behavior they follow, and punishing consequences weaken the behavior they follow.

Consequent events also must be analyzed when caregivers are attempting to decrease a problem behavior or increase a positive behavior. By acting without determining whether a consequence will be helpful or harmful in a given situation, caregivers could unintentionally or inadvertently reinforce and/or increase a negative behavior they are trying to decrease. For example, if parents respond to their child's tantrums by giving in to her demands for a possession, or by ignoring the child and not interacting with her, both responses may increase the likelihood that the child will throw a tantrum again in similar situations. And remember that the relationship between the child's behavior and the environment is bi-directional. So, if the parents' giving in or ignoring immediately stops the child's tantrum, they are more likely to respond in the same way in the future. This, in turn, increases the likelihood of even more tantrums because the child learns that she can get what she wants or can avoid her parents by using that behavior. Such is the nature of functional relationships.

On the other hand, identifying and using consequences that will consistently reinforce positive behaviors in the social environment will increase the frequency of the positive behaviors over time. In order to establish and maintain new social skills in a youth, a caregiver must reinforce a youth anytime he or she uses the skill, especially when first teaching the skill. When the youth becomes proficient at using the skill and begins to experience the natural reinforcement that results (e.g., comfort in social situations, better peer acceptance, more effective communication), the caregiver's rewarding of those behaviors becomes less important and can be faded out.

In conducting a functional analysis of a youth's social behavior, caregivers begin by observing and describing the antecedent and consequent events that appear to precede and follow each significant behavior. Between these two descriptions, caregivers can construct a detailed account of the youth's behavior. By analyzing each component (the "ABC's" – Antecedent,

| Antecedent Event | Behavior | Consequent Event |
|---|---|---|
| Billy approaches an adult and asks to go outside and play. The adult says, "No, it is time to get started on your homework." | Billy begins to argue, raise his voice, curse, and complain that the adult is never fair to him. | The adult responds by saying, "Okay, you can go outside, but only for 20 minutes." Billy calms down immediately and goes outside to play. |

*Figure 1*

Behavior, Consequence), a caregiver should obtain a relatively clear picture of: 1) events that appear to be cues for the behavior to occur; 2) consequences that seem to be maintaining the behavior; and 3) the appropriate social skill that should be taught in order to replace the youth's current problem behavior. An example of a functional analysis is provided in Figure 1.

By analyzing this interaction according to a functional analysis model, we could obtain the following information:

1. The situational cue for Billy to begin arguing and cursing appears to be when he is denied a request (or told "No").

2. The consequent event that is likely to maintain the behavior is the adult giving in to Billy's arguing and complaints about fairness, and Billy engaging in an enjoyable activity immediately following the behavior.

3. The two skill areas that should be addressed in this situation are Billy's difficulty with accepting "No" answers and following instructions.

This example illustrates the information that can be obtained through a functional analysis exercise and observation of a youth's social behavior. The critical elements of any behavior pattern are the events that precede and follow the target behavior or skill, and the specific verbal and nonverbal components of the skill.

## Social Skill Components

In a behavioral teaching program, it is important to distinguish between skills and the behaviors that are part of them. Behaviors are individual, discrete, observable acts demonstrated as part of a larger measure of activity. Some behaviors may be so subtle that they are performed unconsciously (such as looking at a person who is talking to you), and may be part of nearly every social skill.

Skills, on the other hand, are sets of related behaviors or components that are designed to produce positive results for the user in defined situations. It is the consistent and generalized use of such skills that constitute social competency (LeCroy, 1983; Spence & Donovan, 1998). It is critical that caregivers become adept at defining, recognizing, teaching, and reinforcing the behavioral elements of social skills.

The elements of social skills are identified and defined through a process called "task analysis" (Cartledge & Milburn, 1980). The essential steps involved in the task analysis of a social skill area are:

1. Specifying the desired outcome or goal

2. Identifying the essential component behaviors of the goal or skill

3. Stating the behavioral elements of the skill in observable terms

4. Sequencing the component behaviors in order of performance.

For example, if a desired outcome for a particular youth is stated as "will comply with instructions," the task analysis process might guide the caregiver to teach the youth to: 1) look at the person giving the instruction; 2) acknowledge that you heard the instruction; 3) get started right away and stay on task; and 4) let the person know when you are done.

It is important when task-analyzing social behavior to remember that the youth is the primary person who needs to comprehend the listing of individual behaviors. Therefore, the analysis of social skills, if it is to be an effective treatment tool and resource, has to be concise and clear, and use objective language. Figure 2 summarizes guidelines for effective task analysis of social skills.

---

### GUIDELINES FOR TASK ANALYSIS

1. The scope of the main task or skill should be kept limited.

2. Subtasks (behaviors) should be written in observable terms.

3. Terminology should be at a level understood by the potential user.

4. The task should be written in terms of what the learner will do.

5. The task, not the learner, should be the focus of attention.

(Moyer & Dardig, 1978)

---

*Figure 2*

Deficits in social functioning can be measured and assessed in numerous ways. The primary methods of formal assessment, mainly in populations of younger children, include sociometric measures, naturalistic observation and recording, and teacher/caregiver ratings (Gresham, 1981; Oden, 1980). These techniques are primarily designed to produce ratings of peer acceptance, popularity, and social integration that can be correlated with other characteristics of children who score particularly low or high on these measures.

Once skill deficits are observed and defined, caregivers can choose appropriate alternative skills to teach as substitutes. This is accomplished

most effectively on an individual, prescriptive basis for each youth. However, some generalities can be made in order to demonstrate how the choice of opposite competing skills is targeted. Sterba and Dowd (1998) identified a list of possible replacement skills that could be taught as part of treatment for conduct-disordered youth. Their list is summarized in Figure 3.

The process of developing skill-based interventions for youth with difficult behavioral problems is initially dependent on the caregiver's ability to clearly specify and target areas that need remediation and frequent teaching. Agreement then needs to be reached regarding what skills constitute "behavioral opposites" and how they will be taught. For example, if one youth accompanies another in a shoplifting episode, and some caregivers are teaching the skill of "Being Honest" while others are teaching "Resisting Peer Pressure," the youth may not receive the intended benefits in either area.

## Summary

The fundamental elements of a youth's social behavior and skills include the context or situational variables in which they occur, the behavioral components that the youth is capable of performing, and the consequent events that affect future performance. Also, in order for the youth to become socially "competent," he or she needs to be capable of recognizing the subtle social cues of others in the course of an interaction and making appropriate behavioral adjustments.

In the Boys Town programs, a comprehensive curriculum of social skills guides staff members' instructional interactions and treatment planning. This curriculum is presented in Chapter 7. Each skill is task-analyzed and later grouped according to related behavior problem areas and relevant situations (see Appendices C and D) in order to augment the treatment planning process for serious youth issues or special populations.

# Replacement Skills for Conduct-Disordered Youth

| | |
|---|---|
| Following Instructions | Structured Problem-Solving |
| Accepting Consequences | Dealing with Accusations |
| Accepting "No" for an Answer | Dealing with Frustrations |
| Accepting Criticism | Expressing Feelings Appropriately |
| Anger Control Strategies | Negotiating with Others |
| Listening to Others | Problem-Solving a Disagreement |
| Positive Self-Statements about Others | Assertiveness |
| Compromising with Others | Conflict Resolution |
| Controlling Emotions | Accepting Decisions of Authority |
| Coping with Anger and Aggression from Others | Communicating Honestly |
| Self-Monitoring and Reflection | Keeping Property in Its Place |
| Expressing Concern and Understanding for Others | Interacting Appropriately with the Opposite Sex |
| Relaxation Strategies | Waiting Your Turn |
| Making Restitution | Showing Respect |
| Seeking Positive Attention | Getting Teacher's Attention |
| Disagreeing Appropriately | Care for Others' Property |
| Showing Sensitivity to Others | Controlling the Impulse to Steal |
| Following Rules | Use of Appropriate Language |
| Interrupting Appropriately | Making New Friends |
| Making an Apology | |

*Figure 3*

# CHAPTER 3
# Individual Teaching Techniques

When teaching skills to children and adolescents, how the skills are taught is often as important as what is being taught. In other words, caregivers must have an effective, structured method for helping youth learn new skills, improve on existing skills, and become proficient at choosing the right skills to use in specific situations.

The teaching methods that will be covered in this chapter are integral parts of the Boys Town Teaching Model, and are effective in helping children and youth build a repertoire of skills in a variety of settings. By using components such as modeling, demonstration, role-playing, giving feedback, practice, and activities to promote generalization, these teaching approaches work together to prevent inappropriate youth behavior, reinforce positive behavior, and correct negative behavior.

Many children who lack critical skills may not have had the benefit of growing up in an environment where positive social behavior was taught or reinforced. The adults present may not have modeled appropriate styles of interacting with others and the local peer culture or neighborhood may not have valued these positive behaviors. A child, therefore, may have not received any direct instruction in appropriate ways to get his or her immediate needs fulfilled, as is typical in most functional family settings (Oden, 1980).

The lack of reinforcement for important social skills may be a particularly critical feature in the learning histories of children with serious behavioral and emotional problems. For exam-ple, Patterson (1982) and his colleagues found that parents of children who were later described as having aggressive behavior problems were more likely to: 1) use harsh commands and demands with their children; 2) reward negative behaviors with attention or compliance; and 3) ignore, or even punish, prosocial behaviors that their children demonstrated at home. New data point to other negative or antisocial behavior on the part of parents, as well. These children, then, are more likely to act out aggressively in conflict situations at school and with peers, and to be deficient in critical social skill areas such as compliance with rules, problem-solving strategies, and communication skills. While one task of the caregiver – child-care treatment provider, educator, parent, etc. – may be confronting inappropriate behaviors that occur, another simultaneous task is to encourage and motivate the child to replace those behaviors with more socially adaptive responses.

Before we discuss the teaching methods, let's look at two factors that set up successful teaching: specifying behaviors and identifying what skills to teach.

## Specifying Behaviors

A key ingredient in any instructional interaction with a child is being specific. This means that behaviors and skills that are being taught are clearly defined, and even demonstrated for the child, reducing the potential for confusion as much as possible. Chapter 2 referred to the specific elements of appropriate social behavior and task analysis. This same degree of being specific and objective must be reflected in the verbal interactions between adults and the youth they work with or care for.

There are numerous advantages to teaching social skills in a clear, concrete manner. The overall effectiveness of an adult's instruction increases dramatically as the language used becomes more specific and objective. Youth are more likely to learn the components of social skills and, once learned, are more likely to generalize those skills to other situations in which it would be appropriate to use them (school, home, on the job, etc.). This may be particularly critical for those youth with cognitive or learning problems. For example, a learning-disabled child may have particular difficulty understanding vague instructions from teachers or caregivers, recognizing and interpreting the social cues of others, and choosing the appropriate social response in a given situation (Cruickshank, Morse, & Johns, 1980). Clear descriptions and demonstrations of behaviors and skills may help these youth learn more efficiently and, subsequently, handle difficult or ambiguous social situations more successfully.

The process of describing skill components specifically and objectively also may enhance the quality of adult-youth relationships and build trust. Many youth, especially those in treatment programs or institutions, have been told repeatedly what not to do or have been "put down" for the problems they may have.  But when adults take the time to instruct youth in a positive, objective manner, focusing on the skills to use in situations that have caused them difficulties in the past, they are communicating care and concern for the youth in a tangible way. As a result, the youth become more open to the adults' teaching and intervention and are more likely to try out the new skills and behaviors they have been taught. This is especially true when adults are careful to avoid judgmental and value-laden words ("that was wrong," "bad," "stupid," or

"terrible") that may emotionally harm a child or trigger a negative reaction.

# Identifying What Skills to Teach

The practical application of individual teaching techniques for building skills begins with identifying what skills should be taught to a youth. In terms of content and sequencing, individual teaching sessions can focus on: 1) a progression of skills from basic to more advanced; 2) skills specifically identified to be relevant to the youth's most critical treatment issues or needs; 3) preparation for a specific set of circumstances or event; or 4) all of the above. An important consideration in this process is that the youth begins to see the value in the skills that are to be taught (LeCroy, 1983). If the youth sees appropriate skills as meaningful only to the adults who are teaching them, he or she is much less likely to internalize and generalize those skills. That is why it is so critical that the teaching process that is used to train the youth in a new set of skills includes steps that explain the personal benefits of learning such skills.

For the most part, the choice of which particular skills to teach a youth varies with the youth's immediate needs and long-term treatment goals (if applicable). Skills and teaching methods also should always be appropriate for a child's age and developmental level. Once the skills have been identified and prioritized, an adult can map out a strategy that defines how best to teach necessary skills, reinforce their use, and promote internalization and generalization for long-term benefits.

# Opportunities for Teaching and Reinforcing Skills

In almost every child-care or educational setting, there are essentially three situations in which skill instruction takes place. They are:

- When a youth is observed using a skill appropriately (or using an approximation of a skill)

- When preparing or reminding a youth to use a skill in an upcoming situation

- When a youth's inappropriate behavior must be corrected and an alternative appropriate behavior must be taught

The three teaching methods – Effective Praise, Proactive Teaching, and Corrective Teaching – we will discuss in the next few pages have been developed to meet the needs of youth and those adults who work with youth in these situations. The beauty of these methods is that they can be modified and adapted to meet the needs of almost any youth in almost any situation and in almost any setting – schools, shelters, residential programs, treatment facilities, foster care homes, private care programs, and others.

While these methods are essential in providing structure for teaching to youth, there will always be times when informal teaching occurs. Teaching through modeling appropriate behaviors, discussing with youth events where someone used either an appropriate or an inappropriate behavior, and having informal conversations about routine matters all are opportunities for caregivers to help youth expand, enhance, and strengthen their skill base.

# Effective Praise

Everyone likes praise. We want people to tell us when they notice we've done something well or accomplished a goal. Getting a pat on the back or a word of congratulations makes us feel good, both about what we've done and who we are.

This is especially true for children. Whether it's coloring a picture, studying hard for a test, or holding the door open for someone at the grocery store, kids love it when an adult notices they've used or tried to use a positive behavior.

Some of the children with whom you work may rarely have heard those important words of encouragement and praise. They may have been bombarded with criticism plenty of times, and at times, may have been physically punished for their misdeeds. And the times when these kids have tried to do the right thing or have found success, it may have been ignored or treated like it's nothing special.

The children in your care may be hungry for praise. As an important part of a child's treatment or education, praise nurtures emotional growth and provides motivation for youngsters to learn new skills. It is also one of the key elements to building a warm, healthy relationship with kids. Giving praise shows that you genuinely care, that you will take the time to notice when a boy or girl does well, and that you are proud of each child's accomplishments and efforts. Consistently "catching 'em being good" also builds self-confidence in youth, enhances learning, and helps kids to like themselves. Eventually, youth begin to realize that they should use certain behaviors and skills simply because it's the right thing to do.

The best kind of praise is praise that is sincere, natural, and effective. By sincere we mean that youth understand that you are giving praise because you are pleased with what they've done, not just because it's part of your job or because you want them to do something. Praising children naturally means responding spontaneously in a positive way as part of your life. Sometimes, caregivers mistakenly think that praise situations have to be planned out, or that they are "episodes" that are separate from the daily routine. When that happens, caregivers can come across as "mechanical" and children don't see the praise as being sincere. The way to measure praise's effectiveness is by watching whether a child who is praised for a specific behavior continues to use the behavior. If he or she does, it's a good indicator that praise motivates the child and that he or she will try to repeat the behavior because it earns a positive response.

Although frequent general praise creates a nurturing atmosphere, there are times when praise needs to be more specific. (By general praise, we mean brief comments or statements – "Nice job!" "Way to go!" "All right!" – that adults use to informally recognize a youth's appropriate behavior.) At Boys Town, we've developed a teaching approach called Effective Praise, a step-by-step method to ensure that youth get clear messages about their positive behavior. Effective Praise is a way for caregivers to let youth know exactly what they did and why they should continue it, and then to give a positive consequence.

# Steps of Effective Praise

Effective Praise has five steps. All caregivers should use all five steps when they first start working with youth. Later on, as caregivers become more comfortable with giving praise in this manner and have made it a natural part of their everyday contact with youth, a step or two may be left out. The point to remember when using Effective Praise is that praise must be sincere, and that children must understand why they are being praised.

The five steps are:

1. **Give brief praise** – This can be short, enthusiastic words or expressions of praise that let the child know that you recognize he or she has done something well.

2. **Describe the appropriate behavior** – Specifically describe what the youth did, and if the situation calls for it, label the skill he or she used (followed instructions, greeted someone, accepted a "No" answer).

3. **Give a reason for using the behavior** – This helps children make the connection between what they say or do and the possible outcomes or results of their actions.

4. **Ask for acknowledgment** – Make sure the youth understands the reason for using the behavior and why he or she should continue using it.

5. **Give a positive consequence** – The youth earns a positive consequence, which usually is some kind of reward; again, label the skill and specifically describe the behaviors as you tell the youth what he or she earned.

Here's what Effective Praise might sound like when a caregiver in a shelter program sees that a youth has followed an instruction to clean off the dinner table.

1. **Give brief praise** – *"All right! Look at this guy go."*

2. **Describe the appropriate behavior** – *"Jimmy, you did a great job of following instructions. You not only cleaned off all the dishes and silverware and took them to the sink, but you also put the leftovers in the refrigerator. And you did that on your own."*

3. **Give a reason for using the behavior** – *"When you follow instructions to complete chores like this, it helps keep the kitchen in order and shows us that we can count on you to take on responsibilities."*

4. **Ask for acknowledgment** – *"Do you understand why it's good for you to follow instructions when something needs to be done?"*

5. **Give a positive consequence** – *"Thanks for your help. For cleaning off the table and putting away the leftovers, you've earned a half hour of playing video games tonight."*

Here's another example that shows how Effective Praise can be adapted for different settings and situations. In this example, a teacher praises a usually shy fourth-grade student for participating in a class discussion.

1. **Give brief praise** – *"Celia, I wanted to let you know that I was very pleased with your participation in class today."*

2. **Describe the appropriate behavior** – *"You raised you hand almost every time I asked a question, and when I called on you, you gave clear answers that were full of good information."*

3. **Give a reason for using the behavior** – *"When you participate in class like that, you help yourself and the other students learn. And you show that you are paying attention and really thinking about what we are discussing."*

4. **Ask for acknowledgment** – *"Does that make sense?"*

5. **Give a positive consequence** – *"Great job in class today! For participating so well, you can help me hand out the markers and paper for our art hour."*

As well as Effective Praise works, it should not totally take the place of more general praise that can be given anytime. Simply telling youth, "That's great!" "Good job," or "Wonderful work!" can go a long way toward letting them know that their efforts are recognized and appreciated. This is especially true when youth use a specific skill or behavior frequently. When kids know they're doing something correctly and seem pleased with themselves for doing it, a simple "Thanks" may be all that is necessary to acknowledge the positive behavior.

# When to Use Effective Praise

Sometimes, the hardest part about using Effective Praise is remembering to do it and remembering to do it often. Unfortunately, our society "trains" people to focus on the negative aspects of a situation rather than the positive. An example of this is what is known in the restaurant business as the "3-11" rule. This rule states that if you have a good dining experience, you will tell three people about it, but if you have a bad dining experience, you will tell eleven people. In other words, we tend to emphasize the negative over the positive.

It is easy to see when someone makes a mistake or does something wrong. But as a caregiver working with children who have not learned the "right" way to do many things, it is just as important to praise positive behavior as it is to correct negative behavior. Focusing your attention on what a child does well or his or her attempts to do the right thing may require you to change some of your behaviors and attitudes. This is yet another challenge of working with children.

At Boys Town we have discovered a simple truth – praise works wonders. But some adults say that even when they praise children, it doesn't seem to work. Usually, we find that these adults are praising only the biggest achievements or momentous occasions. Once they begin to consistently notice and praise the little things, as well as the big things, their children are doing, they begin to see positive behavior changes. Never underestimate the power of praise.

This raises the question: Should we praise children for every positive behavior, even what they are supposed to do? The answer is "Yes." Children like praise, and the more often they receive it for even the simplest tasks – putting their clothes in the laundry basket, turning off the lights when they leave a room, bringing in the mail – the more likely they are to repeat those activities. Praise feeds a child's desire to succeed. Here are three areas to concentrate on when deciding what you should praise:

■ **When youth use behaviors they already do well or that you want them to continue to use**. Often, adults don't see any reason to praise youth for things they do right; kids are just expected to make appropriate choices. However, it is not always easy for kids to make good decisions; when it happens, it is an extremely positive accomplishment. Giving credit for a youth's success to his or her own effort and ability, and providing encouragement that similar success can be expected in the future, can give a youth something to be proud of, even when he or she misses the mark while attempting new skills.

■ **Improvements in behavior, even small ones.** Praise any effort a youth makes to choose and use positive skills and behaviors. Recognizing and rewarding a step in the right direction helps keep youth motivated to work hard and strengthens your relationship with them.

■ **When youth are learning new skills and making positive attempts to use them.** Provide reinforcement every time a child uses a new skill correctly. This can help kids develop skills more quickly and increase the probability that they will use those skills again. Don't be surprised if kids become frustrated the first few times they try to use a new skill. This is natural. (Think about the first time you tried to begin an exercise or diet program, repair a broken appliance, or wallpaper a room.) That's why kids need a great deal of encouragement. Once a new skill is learned and mastered, the amount of encouragement can be reduced.

It is sometimes very difficult for children to learn new skills. When they try to learn something new, praise the effort. Praising positive attempts to learn or try new skills and other improvements with enthusiasm will carry over to many other areas of children's lives. Make the most of every opportunity to praise kids' positive attempts to learn.

Effective Praise is a teaching tool that recognizes and rewards youth for using skills and specific positive behaviors, increasing the likelihood that they will use those behaviors in the future. Praise helps build positive relationships with kids, while helping them to begin feeling good about themselves and their accomplishments. When Effective Praise is used frequently, kids will become more positive and be more receptive to your teaching and/or treatment.

# Proactive Teaching

Is it better to correct and teach a child not to touch a hot stove after she has burned her hand on it, or to teach her ahead of time that touching a hot stove can hurt her and that she shouldn't go near it?

Obviously, teaching a child how to prevent or avoid a potentially harmful situation would be better than letting the child get hurt before teaching takes place. When it comes to preparing and helping children learn how to respond to the many situations they will face, prevention is the key! This is the idea behind the Boys Town method called Proactive Teaching.

Proactive Teaching is a way for adults to introduce new skills, reinforce skills youth are learning, and to prepare youth for future situations where they will need to use certain skills or behaviors. This is similar to how a coach prepares his team or players for an upcoming game. This teaching occurs during planned, neutral times, when kids are not upset or being corrected, and when the adult (parent, teacher, staff member, etc.) and the youth can both concentrate on what is being taught and learned.

Proactive Teaching is so important to the care and treatment of children because, as we have said, many youth have not yet learned even the basic skills that are needed to function and be successful in society. Normally, children begin learning these basic skills – "Following Instructions," "Getting Along with Others," "Accepting 'No' for an Answer," "Accepting Criticism," and others – at an early age from their parents and other significant adults in their lives. Adult caretakers model certain behaviors, show and tell children how to do skills and when to use them, and continually help children practice, either formally or informally, to help them get better at using those skills.

Many kids don't always have those invaluable learning experiences. They may not know things like how to solve problems without getting angry, how to ask for something politely, or how to share. These skill deficits often have landed them in trouble and have added to the frustration and anger they feel when they are not able to get what they want or need, or accomplish a goal.

In addition to introducing new skills and reinforcing ones that youth already know how to do, Proactive Teaching is vital in helping children achieve "generalization." Generalization, a skill in itself, is the ability to adapt a specific skill to a variety of antecedents, situations, or circumstances. (See Chapter 4 for more on generalization.) For example, a youth who can proficiently use the skill of "Following Instructions" at home, at school, and at swimming practice has learned how to "generalize" the skill to different situations and people. As caregivers, the ultimate goal is for kids to be able to think for themselves, make good decisions, and follow through with appropriate, prosocial behaviors, *on their own*. Proactive Teaching is the training ground where children learn how to do that.

As with all our teaching methods, Proactive Teaching should become a natural part of the care you provide for children. An adult's biggest challenge here is to recognize what needs to be taught, when it needs to be taught, how best to teach it, and how to determine whether a youth is learning.

# The Steps of Proactive Teaching

Proactive Teaching has seven steps. When it is first used with new youth and with youth who are learning new skills, all seven steps should be used in each teaching session. As youth become more skilled, adults may choose to modify their teaching to fit a child's individual needs and situation. This might mean briefer teaching sessions because youth are already familiar with a skill and are getting better at using it. The steps are listed here and an explanation and example of each follows. (In the example, a staff member with a child-care program is working with a program youth.)

1. **Give initial praise.**
2. **Identify the skill and give examples.**
3. **Describe the appropriate behavior (give the skill steps).**
4. **Give a rationale (reason)/Request acknowledgment.**
5. **Practice.**
   **Give feedback.**
   **Give a positive consequence.**
6. **Schedule a follow-up practice.**
7. **Offer praise and encouragement throughout.**

1. **Give initial praise.**

The best way to begin a teaching session is on a positive note. Specifically and sincerely praise any aspect of a child's behavior that is appropriate to the situation. Starting the teaching positively establishes an atmosphere where the child is more likely to listen, participate, and learn.

**Example:** *"Thanks for taking a few minutes to talk with me, Sam."*

2. **Identify the skill and give examples.**

Begin the next step by clearly labeling and explaining the skill. Review a number of specific ways the skill can be used and give the youth plenty of opportunities to ask clarifying questions. Also describe how the skill can be used in a variety of situations and settings; this shows the child that it can be applied to a variety of antecedent conditions or settings.

**Example:** *"Sam, I want to talk with you about a skill that will really help you here while you're in this program, at home, on the job, and in school. It's called 'Following Instructions.' You may get instructions from staff members here and from your teachers at school. And when you go home, I'm sure your mom will have instructions she will want you to follow."*

### 3. Describe the appropriate behavior (give the skill steps).

In this step, specifically describe the behaviors that make up the skill. Demonstrating the skill is a good way to describe it, and a demonstration may be necessary for younger children or youth at lower developmental levels.

**Example:** *"When someone gives you an instruction, Sam, you should look at the person, and with a pleasant voice say something like 'Okay' or 'Sure.' Then, do the task right away. When you're done, check back with the person by saying something like 'Okay, I'm done. Is there anything else?' That would be the best way to follow instructions."*

Again, you might need to demonstrate the skill to ensure that the youth understands. Demonstrations are especially helpful in communicating body posture, voice tone, facial expressions, and other behaviors that are difficult to describe verbally.

### 4. Give a rationale (reason)/Request acknowledgment.

A rationale for learning the skill is next, along with a request for a verbal acknowledgment from the youth. Here, you are asking the youth if he or she understands why it is important to use the particular skill.

**Example:** *"Sam, when you are able to follow instructions from staff members, teachers, or your parents really well, you may have more time to do the things you want to do. Do you understand?"*

### 5. Practice (give feedback and a positive consequence).

After describing the behavior and providing a rationale, have the youth practice the skill. Practicing helps youth become more comfortable with the skill and allows adults to determine the clarity and quality of their teaching up to this

point. After the youth practices, provide feedback in the form of sincere, descriptive praise for all appropriate behaviors, along with a positive consequence for the practice session.

**Example:**

**Staff member:** *"Let's practice just to make sure you got it. Let's pretend I'm your mom at home. When I give you an instruction, look at me, say, 'Okay, I'll get on that,' pretend to do the task, then let me know you are done. Are you ready?"*

**Staff member (playing mom):** *"Sam, will you go finish cleaning your room?"*

**Sam:** *"Okay, I'll get on that right now."* **(Youth pretends to clean room.)** *"I'm done with my room. Is there anything else?"*

**Staff member:** *"Fantastic, Sam! When I gave you that instruction, you looked at me, used a pleasant voice tone, and said, 'Okay, I'll get on that right now.' Then, you pretended to do the task and checked back with me when you were done. You have done an outstanding job of practicing and learning the new skill of 'Following Instructions'! For practicing the skill, you have earned a positive consequence of having an extra snack."*

### 6. Schedule a follow-up practice.

Teaching is further reinforced through a series of follow-up practice sessions. Ideally, the first practice should occur shortly after the teaching session (5 to 15 minutes). Other practices can be done later in the day or evening.

**Example:** *"It's important that we practice the skill of 'Following Instructions' again real soon. Let's practice in about 15 minutes, okay?"*

To further help the youth succeed in these follow-up sessions, prompt him or her before the extra practice. The prompt reminds the youngster of the skill that was practiced earlier and may include having him or her briefly describe the appropriate behaviors that make up the skill.

After each practice, continue to provide descriptive praise, descriptions of the appropriate behavior, and positive consequences. Over time, prompts can be faded out as youngsters show that they can remember and demonstrate the skill consistently.

### 7. Offer praise and encouragement throughout.

Throughout your teaching it is important to provide specific, ongoing praise to the youth. The teaching should end as it began – positively – with praise for the youth's participation and recognition of the appropriate behaviors the youth displayed during the interaction.

**Example:** *"Thanks for taking the time to practice with me. You looked at me during the entire session, stayed on task, and asked some good questions to help you understand what I meant."*

## Preventive Prompt

A special type of Proactive Teaching is the preventive prompt. A preventive prompt is a brief reminder or statement about the use of a skill just before a situation in which the child will use the skill. This is like a coach reminding one of her players about how to run a specific play before sending the player into a game. An adult can use visual, verbal, or physical cues to remind youth what skill they are expected to use and to provide encouragement and reinforcement. A good example of a preventive prompt would be asking a youth, "Do you remember the steps to following instructions?" just before asking him to empty the dishwasher. Preventive prompts are a quick, easy way to help children remember appropriate behaviors and prevent inappropriate behaviors.

## When to Use Proactive Teaching

Proactive Teaching can be done privately with one youth or in small groups. Adults can focus on teaching basic social skills or advanced treatment-oriented skills, preparing a youth for a specific set of circumstances, or "troubleshooting" a youth's skill deficits. When you first begin working with a youth, there should be a heavy emphasis on Proactive Teaching. However, we encourage adults to continue to use this teaching technique whenever necessary.

In a treatment or school setting, one of the first Proactive Teaching sessions might include teaching youth rules and routines, how they work, and why they are important. Early sessions also can focus on an explanation of the basic skills that are needed to be successful in a program, at school, within one's family, and in one's community.

Once this basic information is communicated to a youth, the youth can be introduced to skills that have been identified as ones that he or she needs to learn or work on. As mentioned earlier, basic skills usually are taught first. Examples of basic skills to be taught include "Following Instructions," "Accepting Criticism," "Accepting 'No' for an Answer," "Accepting a Consequence," "Making a Request," and "Disagreeing Appropriately." Proactively teaching these basic skills helps the youth become more open to and comfortable with the process of learning new skills. These basic skills should be taught to every child; they are the building blocks to successfully learning advanced skills.

Often, the process of learning new skills is reinforcing in and of itself, both for youth and adults. In effect, it is easier to teach youth once they've acquired the basic skills.

Most children receive a gradual education in basic and advanced skills from their parents and other adults through modeling, discussion, praise, and discipline. But as we mentioned earlier, many youth typically have not been part of this natural, prosocial education process. In fact, these youth may have received an inconsistent and often dysfunctional education that has left them confused and socially inept. Frequent, specific Proactive Teaching is critical if these youngsters are to make up for lost time and lost opportunities.

Caregivers also can use Proactive Teaching when they are helping with a specific skill or behavior that is giving a youth problems. Often, this type of skill deficit can escalate and lead to a loss of self-control. Proactive Teaching can help reduce the chances of an emotional response. For example, if a youth consistently becomes verbally or physically aggressive and loses self-control when given a "No" answer, Proactive Teaching sessions should focus on the skill of "Accepting 'No' for an Answer."

Proactive Teaching builds relationships and fosters skill development. It can be used to teach youth basic and advanced social skills, prepare youth for specific situations or circumstances, and "troubleshoot" specific skill deficiencies. Proactive Teaching can be done on an individual basis or with the entire group of youth, depending on the circumstances. Proactive Teaching is a real key to youth success and to a caregiver's sense of accomplishment.

# Corrective Teaching

While an important goal is to praise children for using appropriate skills and behaviors whenever possible, and to prepare them for situations where they will have to use certain skills, there will be times when you have to correct a child's misbehavior.

As a caregiver, you are responsible for helping children learn new appropriate behaviors and skills that can be used to replace past problem behaviors. These new skills assist younger children in their normal development as they grow through adolescence, and help adolescents as they grow into adulthood. When kids are directly and consistently taught new ways of behaving, they can more successfully and comfortably adapt to societal norms and get their needs met in more acceptable ways.

Direct, frequent, consistent, and concerned teaching also helps caregivers. A structured teaching approach provides a specific, effective, and positive way to deal with problem behaviors. Because teaching is a positive intervention that works well and is liked by children, you can avoid punitive approaches that would damage relationships.

At Boys Town, we have developed a teaching method called Corrective Teaching for dealing with problem behaviors and teaching more appropriate replacement behaviors. By thoughtfully and consistently using Corrective Teaching, you can help each child recover from the past and grow into the future.

## Steps of Corrective Teaching

Corrective Teaching is a structured method for responding when a child misbehaves or fails to do something he or she should do. Through Corrective Teaching, adults teach alternative appropriate skills to replace a child's negative responses to situations and people around him or her. This teaching also allows caregivers to share their experiences, knowledge, and abilities to help kids learn and grow socially and emotionally.

This proven teaching method consists of nine steps and is characterized by three central concepts – description, relationship, and consequence. Description involves specifically describing a behavior through words or actions, role-playing, and practice. The relationship concept involves using warmth and pleasantness, and showing genuine concern for the youth. It also focuses on helping the child to learn how to develop healthy relationships with others. Consequences include giving feedback and practice, and having a youth lose a privilege or something he or she likes for using an inappropriate behavior. For teaching to be effective, there must be a balance among these three concepts.

Let's take a closer look at the nine steps and their definitions:

1. **Give initial praise or empathy.**

2. **Describe or demonstrate the inappropriate behavior.**

3. **Give a negative consequence.**

   Positive correction statement

4. **Describe or demonstrate the appropriate behavior (give the skill steps).**

5. **Give a rationale (reason).**

6. **Request acknowledgment.**

7. **Practice.**

8. **Give feedback.**

   Praise

   Positive consequence (up to half of the negative consequence)

9. **Offer praise and encouragement throughout.**

**1. Give initial praise or empathy.**

This begins teaching on a positive note. Using a statement of empathy (e.g., "I know this is hard for you.") lets kids know that you care and want to help. Praise statements (e.g., "Thanks for coming over right away to talk with me.") recognize the child for using a positive behavior. Both kinds of statements are excellent ways to prevent a youngster from reacting with volatile behaviors to your upcoming teaching and consequence.

**2. Describe or demonstrate the inappropriate behavior.**

The description of what the child did incorrectly should be simple and brief so that the child can understand it. For some kids, especially younger children and youth at lower developmental levels, a demonstration may be necessary. A word of caution: Spending too much time on the description of the misbehavior can come across as "nagging," which can trigger a loss of self-control from youngsters.

**3. Give a negative consequence.**

This step involves having a youth lose something that is meaningful to him or her for using the inappropriate behavior. When consequences are given, it is important that children understand that their behavior earned the consequence and that they are responsible for that behavior. After the consequence is given, tell the child that he or she will have a chance to earn back part of the consequence (no more than half) for practicing an alternative appropriate skill with you. This is called a "positive correction statement," and it gives kids hope that all is not lost.

**4. Describe or demonstrate the appropriate behavior (give the skill steps).**

In this step, give a simple and brief explanation of the skill or behavior the youngster should use in place of the inappropriate behavior. If necessary, go over the steps to a specific skill or demonstrate the specific behavior you want the youth to use in a similar situation. You also can help the youth generalize the skill or behavior to other situations by saying something like, "When an adult you know and trust asks you to (name the skill or behavior), you should...." Again, it is important to make sure your words or demonstration match the child's age and developmental level.

**5. Give a rationale (reason).**

This step is where you tell youth why they should change their behavior. In a sense, it's where you "sell" the skill to kids. Generally speaking, younger children and kids who are new to teaching respond best to rationales that let them know the personal benefits of using the new behavior. A rationale that explains the negative consequences of continuing to use the old inappropriate behavior also works with these kids. With older youth and youngsters who are familiar with your teaching, "other-centered" rationales usually work best. These rationales let kids know how using a new skill or behavior will benefit others. Here, caregivers are helping kids move away from thinking only of themselves to thinking about how their behaviors and actions affect others. As a result, kids begin to learn and develop morals and positive values.

**6. Request acknowledgment.**

After giving a rationale, ask youth if they understand it and what is being taught. If a child doesn't understand the rationale, patiently give another one. It's important not to move on to the next step until the child lets you know that he or she understands what you are teaching. Requests for acknowledgment can be used anytime during teaching when a youth appears confused.

**7. Practice.**

Here, the youth is given an opportunity to use the new skill or behavior in a pretend situation. Make sure to set up the practice clearly so that he or she isn't confused about what to do. The best practices are ones that are somehow related to the child's original inappropriate behavior. (Avoid practices that might come across as contrived or silly; for example, don't say, "Billy, please pick up that pencil," when practicing the skill of "Following Instructions" because Billy didn't take out the garbage when asked.) Practice is important because it gives the child a chance to be successful and gain confidence before he or she has to use the skill or behavior in a real-life situation.

**8. Give feedback.**

Following the practice, tell the youth how well he or she did using the new behavior or skill. This provides an opportunity for youth to "fine-tune" their new behaviors and skills. Depending on the situation, you may have the youth practice again or simply point out anything that was left out and remind him or her to include it the next time the skill is used. After the practice and feedback, kids can earn back up to half of the negative consequence (positive cor-

rection) given earlier. For example, if a youth's consequence is losing a half hour of playing outside, he or she could earn back a maximum of 15 minutes of playing outside for practicing and accepting feedback. Positive correction is a powerful incentive for getting kids to take practicing seriously and not give up when the negative consequence is delivered.

**9. Offer praise and encouragement throughout.**

This ends teaching on a positive note by recognizing and praising a youngster's efforts to learn and practice a new behavior. Praising and encouraging kids at this time and throughout the interaction helps take their focus away from the negative consequence and allows them to leave the teaching session feeling good about themselves.

# Corrective Teaching Example

Let's take a look at an example of what Corrective Teaching might look and sound like when teaching the skill of "Compromising with Others."

Tim, 14, and Dwayne, 13, are residents of a group home. During free time, Tim and Dwayne begin to argue about what TV program to watch. The boys begin shouting at each other and fighting over the remote control. When a staff member hears the ruckus, she tells the boys to stop arguing and sit on the couch. When they comply, she begins Corrective Teaching.

**Staff member:** *"Tim and Dwayne, thanks for stopping your argument and sitting down right away.* (Give initial praise or empathy.) *Let's talk about what just happened. I saw both of you yelling at each other over what channel to watch and fighting over the remote. That is not acceptable behavior."* (Describe or demonstrate the inappropriate behavior.)

**Tim:** *"But Dwayne was hogging the TV. It was my turn, and my favorite show was on."*

**Staff member:** *"I understand that you both really wanted to watch your programs.* (Give praise/empathy.) *But for yelling at each other and fighting, you've both lost an hour of TV time.* (Give a negative consequence.) *Remember, you'll both have a chance to earn some of that time back when we practice.* (Positive correction statement.) *Okay?"*

**Tim and Dwayne nod in acknowledgment.**

**Staff member:** *"Super job of accepting your consequence, Tim and Dwayne!* (Give praise.) *Now, let's talk about how you can settle a disagreement without arguing and fighting. One way is to use the skill of 'Compromising with Others.' Compromising means coming up with a plan that people can agree on when they're having a problem. Next time you have a disagreement with someone, the best way to handle it is to remain calm. Then talk to the other person about what you would like to do and what he would like to do, and suggest something that both of you can agree on. If you aren't able to agree, stay calm and go find an adult to help.* (Describe or demonstrate the appropriate behavior.) *That way, you're more likely to come up with a solution that works for you and the other person, and no one ends up getting hurt.* (Give a rationale.) *Do you understand all that?"* (Request acknowledgment.)

**Tim:** *"Yeah."*

**Dwayne:** *"Yes."*

**Staff member:** *"Now let's practice how to compromise with others. Dwayne, pretend that you're playing a CD on the stereo and Tim comes in to play one of his CDs. Do you both remember the steps to compromising with others?"*

**Tim:** *"Yes."*

**Dwayne:** *"Yes."*

**Staff member:** *"Great. Let's practice what you are going to do and say."*

**Tim (looking at Dwayne):** *"Dwayne, you've been listening to that CD on the stereo for a long time. How about if you let me listen to my CD for a while and you can listen to one of my CDs later."* (Practice.)

**Dwayne:** *"Okay, that would be cool. Can I listen to the CD you just bought?"*

**Tim:** *"Sure. Thanks Dwayne."*

**Dwayne:** *"You're welcome."*

**Staff member:** *"That was fantastic! You both stayed calm and came up with an excellent option. Remember, if both of you aren't able to agree on a solution, continue to stay calm and go find an adult to help out.* (Give feedback.) *Since you did such a great job of practicing this new skill, you've both earned back a half-hour of TV time.* (Give a positive consequence.) *Tim and Dwayne, you did a super job of remaining calm this whole time and working hard with me on learning this new skill. I'm really proud of you!"* (Offer praise and encouragement.)

Corrective Teaching is a proven method for helping youth learn how to use appropriate behaviors in place of inappropriate behaviors. Three concept areas – description, relationship, and consequence – comprise the Corrective Teaching Interaction. Within these areas are nine specific steps that provide structure to the teaching process while also allowing adults to develop and strengthen relationships. The effective use of Corrective Teaching can empower kids to make new behaviors a permanent part of their daily lives and enable them to successfully use these behaviors and skills in many different situations.

# Promoting Generalization during Teaching

Generalization is addressed in more detail in other parts of this book. (See Chapter 4.) When it comes to specific teaching techniques, it is sufficient to say that several components of Proactive Teaching, Effective Praise, and Corrective Teaching are geared to promote the use of skills across situations. The "rationales" component is probably the most important of these. Well-constructed rationales point out to a youth how learning appropriate styles of interacting with others will produce favorable outcomes in other arenas of his or her life (including school, with peers, at home, etc.). However, for rationales to be truly effective in getting a youth to learn and implement new skills, the adults working with that youth must know his or her individual likes and dislikes, values, and experiences very well. Knowledge of what a youth finds important and meaningful in life is critical to fostering the internal motivation to change.

Other specific techniques can be utilized during social skills training in order to increase the potential for generalization and maintenance (Sulzer-Azaroff & Mayer, 1986; Cartledge & Milburn, 1980; Goldstein, Sprafkin, Gershaw, & Klein, 1980). They include:

1. **Teaching in different settings:** This means varying the location of instruction in order to simulate the different situations the youth may encounter. Simultaneously teach the youth to discriminate between situations and successfully identify which skills to use.

2. **Teaching with different people:** This means using more than one caregiver or staff person to define, model, and role-play the target skills with the youth. It is best if persons who are involved with the youth in other stimulus situations can participate (i.e., the youth's teacher or counselor, a parent, peers, etc.).

3. **"Homework" assignments:** These are commonly used in group social skills training (see Chapter 5) or on an outpatient basis. The youth is given an assignment to use a skill in a particular situation, record the outcome, and report back to the adult who is teaching the skill.

4. **Altering reinforcement contingencies:** This approach increases the natural reinforcement for prosocial behavior. Generalization is enhanced when skills that are taught are ones that parents, teachers, and peers will reinforce more often than the youth's inappropriate responses (Howing, Wodarski, Kurtz, & Gaudin, 1990).

It is apparent that a number of activities within a skill-teaching session with a child can and should be used to promote generalization and maintenance. However, in day-to-day interactions with their youth, caregivers should be attuned to the opportunities that are present for rewarding prosocial behavior and correcting inappropriate behaviors that occur. These two processes themselves are critical to the generalization of skills that are taught in planned, structured teaching situations.

# Summary

Teaching children skills and behaviors so that they can change for the better is an awesome responsibility. Every situation you face will pose a different, and often difficult, challenge. Having confidence in your abilities and tools – specifically effective teaching methods – and constantly working to improve how you apply them in your service to youth, will be the key to success for you and the young people in your care.

Everyone who shoulders the responsibility of helping, teaching, or caring for children has some ability to teach new skills and appropriate behaviors. Only when a person applies that ability in a compassionate and competent manner, with the best interests of the youth at heart, can the desired results be achieved – a youth who has learned not only how to behave differently but how to live differently.

# CHAPTER 4
# Generalization of Social Skills

I n effective behavior-change programs, youth (or adults) learn and become proficient at using skills and behaviors, and then are able to use them in many situations inside and outside the instructional setting. In other words, a youth is able to apply what he or she has learned beyond the bounds of the program, with many different people and in many different situations. This is called **generalization**, and it is one of the true measures of the success of social skills training.

**Generalization** means that skills learned under one set of antecedent (or stimulus) conditions are used under different sets of antecedent (stimulus) conditions. For example, a youth who learns and uses the skill of "Following Instructions" at home with his parents, and then can appropriately use the skill with teachers at school, has learned how to generalize that skill to different situations. Generalization is a skill in and of itself, and it helps youth move from simply performing skills to making cognitive choices about when, where, and how to use them.

Generalization of skills and behaviors is achieved through the process of generalization training. Generalization training is a procedure in which a behavior is reinforced in a number of different stimulus situations until the behavior occurs naturally and reliably across settings. Often, behavior-change programs teach a number of socially important skills and behaviors to clients and then expect them to automatically be able to use the skills and behaviors in new situations. Stokes and Baer (1977) call this the "train-and-hope" approach to the generaliza-

tion of skills. Successful generalization training, however, employs active methods like practice and role-playing to ensure that the learner can successfully use socially important behaviors in a number of relevant social contexts.

Before we examine ways to help youth achieve generalization, a key philosophical point must be made. We must realize that when youth do not or cannot generalize skills and behaviors, it is usually due to the failure of adults, not the youth. Youth seldom choose not to use learned skills in different settings. Adults must assume the responsibility when this happens, and must work harder to educate youth in the skill of generalization.

## Generalization Training

Gresham, Sugai, and Horner (2001) cite several likely reasons for the lack of generalization in social skills training. One reason is that skills tend to be taught in artificial situations and often are not reinforced in the youth's natural environment. So, one way to achieve generalization is to train those skills or behaviors that are most likely to be reinforced in the natural environment. This approach is called "trapping" and involves developing behavior that falls into the "behavior trap" represented by what happens in the environment when those behaviors are used (Baer & Wolf, 1970). Social skills such as "Talking with Others," "Accepting Criticism," and "Following Instructions" will probably be socially reinforced by a significant number of people in the youth's environment. The youth is more likely to continue to use these behaviors after the training because natural reinforcers like positive attention and approval by others will reinforce the behaviors.

In terms of the "behavior trap," it is imperative to teach skills that are considered socially valid. The concept of social validity (Wolf, 1978) provides a basis for identifying relevant behaviors to be taught. A skill or behavior is socially valid if it is efficient and reliable. An efficient skill produces the expected outcome with less effort and likely some form of reinforcement. A reliable skill produces the expected outcome or reinforcers consistently. If the newly trained skill of "Talking with Others" leads to increased reinforcement and the desired outcome (peer inclusion), then it is said to be efficient and reliable. Selecting socially valid skills prior to intervention demonstrates how generalization can be programmed into an intervention from the beginning. When possible, parents (or other caregivers) should be involved when determining what social skills would be beneficial to a youth because parents play a critical role in social skill development and generalization (Arthur, Bochner, & Butterfield, 1999).

# Promoting Generalization

Now that we have established the necessity of selecting relevant skills to be taught, what is the best way to teach these skills in order to promote generalization?

Whether or not generalization occurs depends heavily on how similar the different stimulus situations are. The more similar these situations are, the more initial generalization there will be between them. Social skills should be taught in situations that are as similar as possible to the environments in which youth can be expected to use the skills. For example, the skill of "Getting the Teacher's Attention" should be taught in situations that closely simulate a classroom setting because that is where a youth ultimately is going

to use the skill. Research supports the idea that a new behavior can be taught and learned through direct instructional techniques; many times, however, a skill is taught in a contrived setting and has little meaning or utility to a youth outside of that setting (Gresham, 1998). This does not mean a skill cannot be discussed and modeled outside the classroom. But to increase the likelihood that the youth will successfully generalize the skill, it is best to actually practice the skill in a classroom or a classroom-like setting.

Such a generalization teaching approach also should include varying the training conditions when possible, training in different locations, using different instructors, and incorporating pairs or small groups of learners to make the training more realistic. When training takes place in an environment that is different from the actual setting, real-life experiences should be used whenever possible and the training should be related to experiences that occur outside the training environment. This means discussing with youth specifically where, when, and with whom skills may be used.

Social skills training also should include some form of "cognitive mediators." Cognitive mediators incorporate a "how-to-think" component into social skills training. They enable youth to assess how well or how poorly they used a skill, and to think about what, if anything, they should do differently the next time they use the skill. Research indicates that cognitive strategies like this can decrease hyperactivity/impulsivity and disruption/aggression, and strengthen prosocial behavior (Robinson, Smith, Miller, & Brownell, 1999).

Caregivers can implement this element by providing clear expectations, imagery, some form of self-talk, such as a rationale for using the skill, and problem-solving strategies. Generalization is enhanced when there is some form of internal motivation to use the skill. For example, a youth who understands that using a particular skill will help her avoid a negative consequence is more likely to use the skill in a variety of settings. The same may be true for a youth who sees that using the skill of "Following Instructions" helps him complete a task faster and earns him a reputation of being trustworthy. The use of cognitive mediators in social skills training should assist the youth in identifying and interpreting social cues, predicting what may happen next, selecting what skill to use, and evaluating the outcome of using the skill.

To further promote generalization, the final stages of social skills training should involve the use of natural and logical consequences that are very similar to those that will occur in real life. Many programs that teach youth social skills use some form of a motivation system in which youth earn or lose points, tokens, or some other form of consequences, contingent on their behavior. (Boys Town uses a motivation system where youth earn points for appropriate behavior and lose points for inappropriate behavior. When youth have a preset number of points at the end of the day, they can use the points they've earned to purchase privileges and other rewards.)

Ideally, an effective motivation system is paired with praise and other forms of positive attention and approval. This allows caregivers to gradually "fade" a youth off the motivation system and rely on praise, attention, and approval alone to motivate him or her to continue using positive behavior and skills. For example, as a youth in a program learns the skill of "Following Instructions" and improves her proficiency with it, she receives points or tokens for using the skill in applicable situations. The program staff then gradually fades the use of points and increases social praise for the youth's use of the skill. Eventually, the youth will be motivated to continue to use the skill by praise and other forms of approval, the natural and logical consequences she would receive for appropriate behavior at home or school.

The key to any successful social skills training program is what happens when a youth demonstrates a skill spontaneously. When this occurs in a new setting, reinforcement of the behavior should be increased enough to ensure that the youth will consistently maintain the behavior. If a youth fails to use a skill or uses the skill inappropriately, there should be a consistent method of correction, with emphasis on teaching the alternative behavior.

# Summary

In a manner of speaking, generalization is the pot of gold at the end of the social skills training rainbow. When a youth shows that he or she can competently and correctly generalize a skill to a variety of situations, it is a sign of success that the youth has moved to a new level of skill competency.

Generalization is most likely to be achieved when social skills training and practice occur in situations that are as similar as possible to the situations where a youth will be expected to use new skills. Regardless of where youth are learning skills – in a child-service program, at school, in a youth shelter, in a clinical setting, at home – the ultimate goal is to equip youth for social interactions by giving them the skills they need and to prepare them to use those skills in many situations. Social skills training without generalization only provides youth with a list of behaviors that lead to appropriate behavior. Knowing how and when to apply those behaviors is the real key to long-lasting and meaningful change that, in the end, helps kids overcome problems and be successful.

# CHAPTER 5
# Teaching Skills in Group Settings

An alternative way to teach interpersonal skills to children and adolescents is to use a group-teaching format. Bandura (1989) stated that most social learning takes place by observing others and the results of their actions. A group setting provides an immediate social environment in which specific skills can be taught and practiced, and in which a youth can gradually become sensitized to his or her role as a group member. This is an important process because of the numerous "groups" all youth must function in as a part of normal family and community life (school classes, peer groups, sports teams, work groups, etc.).

By incorporating social skills group training into a setting where a child is receiving treatment, education, or other types of care, adults can address individual goals and target areas and effectively teach and maintain skills. In other words, the advantages of a group-teaching format can be applied to each youngster's individual benefit. In this chapter, we will review these advantages, some previous uses of group skills training, a structured format for conducting skills groups, and techniques for maintaining productive group meetings.

## Advantages of Group Teaching

There are many reasons for incorporating skill-building groups into child-care programs and educational settings as a way to augment individual efforts. The group provides a ready-made social setting in which to assess each member's ongoing social functioning under a variety of circumstances, as well as a more natural teaching situation (Trower, Bryant, & Argyle, 1978). The youth's ability to participate in group activities, concentrate on lessons and tasks, and respond to performance demands may give adults valuable insight into potential problems in other situations that would require similar skills (such as being in a classroom).

Because skills-training groups allow several youth to participate together, there is increased opportunity for each member to share his or her responses and differing perspectives to problem situations, and to perhaps generate alternative ways of handling difficult circumstances (Hazel, Schumaker, Sherman, & Sheldon-Wildgen, 1983). This may be especially important for those children with learning or cognitive deficits who tend to rigidly stick to one set of responses in diverse situations. Participation in a group may let children know that there are numerous ways to handle stressful or demanding situations and that their previous strategies represent only one option. Many times, a youth's peers themselves communicate this message most effectively. Several studies with autistic children reveal that involving peers in social skills interventions provides children with autism the opportunity to observe, imitate, and learn from the social behaviors of their typically developing peers (Kamps et al., 2002).

There also is evidence that behaviors and skills learned in a group setting may come under control of a greater number of clearly different stimuli, thus increasing the probability that learned skills will be used in situations outside the group (Howing, Wodarski, Kurtz, & Gaudin, 1990). The result, therefore, would be greater generalization of the specific skills taught in the group to diverse situations that youth face and greater maintenance of these skills following treatment. This is especially true when several different training techniques (as well as different adult trainers) are used to enhance and prompt generalization.

In addition to these benefits, providing skills training in group settings can increase the number of youth who may be served by a particular program or service, or may increase the cost-effectiveness of a program with limited staff or resources. The advantages of conducting skills training in group settings are summarized in Figure 1.

---

### ADVANTAGES OF GROUP SETTINGS

1. Assessment of social functioning in the group

2. Training in more realistic settings

3. Opportunity to share experiences and options

4. Enhanced generalization and maintenance of skills

5. Cost efficient and time efficient

---

*Figure 1*

Group skills training has been used in many treatment settings, schools, and outpatient programs. The populations and age groups that have been served using this format have been extremely varied as well.

One group of youth that has received particular attention in regard to skills training is juvenile delinquents. This is no doubt due to the well-documented relationship between low social skill functioning and delinquent behavior in adolescents and young adults. Several studies have shown the effectiveness of using group teaching techniques with groups of juvenile delinquents. In one report (Shivrattan, 1988), in-

carcerated male delinquents participated in a social skills training program designed to increase cognitive empathy in participants. The results showed that these youth improved on measures of being considerate, insight, and anger control. In addition, a one-year follow-up of the participants revealed that they had lower rates of recidivism and better community adjustment than their counterparts in a control group.

Skills groups also have been conducted with court-adjudicated adolescents on an outpatient basis (Hazel et al., 1983). This typically involves having youth attend a weekly group meeting that lasts 1½ to 2 hours and focuses on a limited number of target skills (e.g., "Following Instructions," "Resisting Peer Pressure," and "Accepting Criticism"). In an evaluation of one such program for court-adjudicated youth, Hazel et al. (1983) demonstrated that this effort also produced lower rates of recidivism for group participants after one year than were evident in a comparison group that did not participate in the training.

Skills-training groups have been used as part of inpatient psychiatric and day-treatment programs for adolescents as well. For example, when conversation skills were taught to inpatient children and adolescents, the result was better communication behaviors demonstrated both with peers and with unfamiliar adults (Hansen, St. Lawrence, & Christoff, 1989). The effects of an improved style of communication can enhance the other therapeutic gains made by each youth within the psychiatric setting.

This also has been considered true for social skills groups conducted as part of day-treatment programming for emotionally disturbed adolescents (Friedman, Quick, Mayo, & Palmer, 1983). In this case, the training resulted in better peer relationships and better conflict resolution within the program, and thus greater gains by the program's participants overall.

Skills intervention based on a group format has been used effectively in educational settings with both handicapped and nonhandicapped youngsters. In-school social skill instruction has been used with disruptive students of all ages in urban and rural high schools to reduce antisocial behavior and discipline referrals. An additional benefit of this approach is a corresponding increase in on-task behavior from students and better performance on curriculum measures. The implication here is that school may, in fact, be the ideal place in which to conduct social skills training groups because the positive effects of training may be more pronounced there anyway.

For many young people, school remains the biggest challenge in their lives. Gresham (1995) notes that schools are one of the most important settings in which children acquire, develop, and refine the skills that are essential for establishing and maintaining interpersonal relationships. By learning new sets of positive, prosocial behaviors within the school environment, students may be more immediately equipped to deal with academic and social obstacles.

# Structure and Format of the Skills Group

In deciding on the structure, scheduling, and content of a skills-training group, a large number of factors must be considered. These include the size and makeup of the group, characteristics of the participants, and decisions regarding who will lead the training exercises. The content of any given session may vary according to the age, developmental level, abilities, and presenting problems of the youth.

Despite the flexibility possible in designing and implementing a skills-training program, a few generalities can be made based on previous experience. For example, small groups of 10 or fewer youth are thought to be more effective with regular instruction occurring at least twice a week (Howing et al., 1990). Using more than

one trainer, preferably a male and a female, also is recommended in order to enhance the potential for generalization and to help monitor the behavior of the participants.

The youths' previous grouping or participation in groups in other primary treatment programs most often determines those youths' characteristics. For example, a social skills group may include all of the children in a particular hospital unit or special education class. In these cases, the group members may already know each other or have formed some friendships. On the other hand, group members may be drawn from the population of young people adjudicated by a county juvenile court for a one-month period. In this case, special activities would be necessary at the outset to introduce group members and make each comfortable with the situation. In both of these examples, however, a positive group atmosphere needs to be created at the outset and maintained by the group leaders.

Ang and Hughes (2001) found that skills-training intervention delivered in the context of groups of only antisocial peers produced smaller benefits than did skills-training interventions that avoided grouping only antisocial peers together. This is critical since the issues under discussion may include alternatives to delinquency or drug behavior, which group members should not glamorize or brag about. (Techniques for maintaining a productive training environment will be covered later in this chapter.)

Issues related to grouping and participant characteristics also include whether to combine groups of children who are different in their functioning level and/or handicap. It is appropriate to combine higher-functioning and lower-functioning children in a social skills training group as long as the behaviors of the higher-functioning children are generally attainable and capable of being modeled and performed by the lower-functioning members (Howing et al., 1990). In fact, the inclusion of nonhandicapped peers into a social skills group for handicapped children is quite positive because the nonhandicapped children's behaviors are more likely to be modeled and imitated, especially if these behaviors result in peer reinforcement (Gresham, 1981).

Prior to beginning a skills-training group, trainers should invest a good deal of time in preparation and planning. The setting should be arranged, materials organized, and reinforcers planned in advance in order to reward positive performance and participation. Additional guidelines for specifically planning instructional content include (Oden, 1980):

1. **Select content focus.** Select the one or two skills that will be covered in that particular session.

2. **Organize the content.** The content and materials should be clearly organized, with particular emphasis on matching the language to be used to the ages and developmental levels of the participants.

3. **Prepare the oral presentation of material.** Plan examples to be used and role-play scenes that can be acted out. Prepare answers to different responses from group members and an explanation of how inappropriate behavior will be addressed.

4. **Select activities for peer interaction and reinforcement.** The skills instruction may be built around normal activities or a special game. The trainer also should plan reinforcing activities for group members at the conclusion of the session.

# Group Teaching Format

The specific components and format of skills training are summarized in Figure 2. A definition of each component and an example of what the component might sound like in a residential treatment program follows. (For ease of presentation, only one leader is conducting the session in the example. Usually, it is best to have two "co-leaders"; other staff members can as-

sist, depending on the size of the group and the activities that are planned.) While a residential treatment program is used in this example, it is important to remember that group training can be used in a variety of settings with a variety of children.

---

### GROUP TEACHING COMPONENTS

1. Start the group session.

2. Introduce the topic or skill.

3. Define and model the skill.

4. Role-play the target skill.

5. Have youth earn positive consequences (Individual/Group).

6. Give a generalization assignment and prompt.

---

*Figure 2*

1. **Start the group session:** The group leader brings the session to order with a clear beginning prompt or cue that is used consistently to start each session. The leader then welcomes the participants and reviews the group rules and the behaviors expected from group members. (See Figure 3 on page 45.)

The group could then review the previous lesson or any assignments that were given at the end of the previous lesson. The leader should also remind group members about the reinforcers or rewards available for positive group participation or skill performance.

**Example**

**Leader:** *"Okay, guys, let's bring this meeting to order. (pause) Good, thanks for quieting down. Before we get started, let's review the rules we established for our group meetings. Tom, can you tell us one?"*

**Tom:** *"Yeah, we raise our hands before talking and don't just call out."*

**Leader:** *"Good, Tom, that's right! Raising our hands will help our meetings be more organized and probably go faster. Does anyone else have a rule they would like to give? If not, then let's see if you have your homework from our last session. Please pass it up front and remember that if you are turning in your assignment, you can earn an extra 15 minutes of game time on the computer. Also, I want to remind you guys that if you work hard on today's skills, you can earn up to a half hour of extra TV time this afternoon. Okay, let's get started."*

2. **Introduce the topic or skill:** Here the group leader introduces the skill or skills that will be the focus of the session. They are stated as a concept and labeled by the name that everyone will consistently call them. Then, the leader talks about situations where the target skill may be used. The leader may give an example of these situations first, then ask for suggestions from the group. This not only promotes more meaningful involvement, but also helps to reinforce the ongoing level of understanding of the group members. The leader also may ask the youth how they have handled these types of situations in the past and whether those responses have resulted in negative consequences.

**Example**

**Leader:** *"We are going to talk today about a skill that will really help you all here in the program and when you go home to your parents. The skill is 'Accepting "No" for an Answer.' This skill has to do with what you might say and do when you want to do something and the person you ask tells you 'No.' For example, if you wanted to go outside and play, you might ask your mom if it's all right to do that. But your mom might say that dinner is almost ready, so the answer is*

*'No.' What are some other times when someone might tell you 'No?'"*

**Bill:** *"I might ask my teacher if I can get a drink and he could tell me 'No.'"*

**Leader:** *"That's a good example, Bill. Tell me what you have done when things like that have happened before?"*

**Bill:** *"I guess I usually got pretty mad and lost my temper."*

**Leader:** *"Okay, and can anybody tell us what could happen if you get mad and lose your temper in school?"*

**Alicia:** *"I know when I've gotten mad like that I usually ended up in the office."*

**Leader:** *"You're right. That could happen. So today we are going to talk about a different way to handle being given a 'No' answer."*

3. **Define and model the skill:** The leader now verbally and visually defines the component behaviors of the target skill. This is first done with a verbal explanation of each step of the skill. During this time, the leader lists any youth responses on chart paper or a chalkboard. The leader then models these behaviors by using a situation based on one of the examples given during the previous step. Modeling a situation can be repeated or several situations can be acted out in order to help the youth understand. The group leader also explains a reason for using the appropriate responses rather than inappropriate ones that may result in negative consequences for the youth. The leader then asks the group members for more examples.

**Example**

**Leader:** *"Whenever you receive a 'No' answer, here's what you should do. First, continue looking at the person you are talking to. Second,* *acknowledge the answer by saying something like 'Okay' or 'Sure, no problem' in a pleasant tone of voice. Third, don't use any behaviors like whining, arguing, or mumbling under your breath. And fourth, if you have a question, ask the person if you can discuss your request later on. If you do those things, you will be accepting a 'No' answer really well. In fact, to show you guys what we're talking about, Alicia and I will practice this skill using Bill's example of asking his teacher if he can get a drink during class."*

**The leader and Alicia model the skill.**

**Leader:** *"Did everyone see what we did here? When I told Alicia 'No' about getting a drink, she continued looking at me, said 'Okay, maybe later,' and did not argue or whine. The reason it is so important to use these behaviors is that the person who told you 'No' this time may be willing to negotiate later on for something else if you can accept the first answer without arguing or becoming aggressive. Does everybody understand that? Can anyone else think of another reason to accept 'No' answers appropriately?"*

**Tom:** *"Maybe because if you get angry you'll just end up in more trouble than you started with."*

**Leader:** *"That's right, Tom. And maybe you will make the other person angry back at you and he or she will be less willing to ever say 'Yes' to you when you want to do something in the future. Does anyone else have a reason for why we should accept 'No' answers like this?"*

4. **Role-play the target skill:** In this step, each youth is given an opportunity to rehearse the behaviors of the target skill several times in order to learn and begin to generalize the component behaviors. This begins with the leader reviewing the components of the skill and then setting up realistic role-play situations, possibly based on earlier examples offered by the youth. Each youth

should first practice the skill with the leader, and then with a peer. The leader follows up each practice with immediate behavioral feedback for the youth by praising the youth's efforts, describing the parts of the role play that were correctly done to criteria, and describing any component behaviors that were left out or not performed to criteria.

While it is important that effective teaching takes place, the emphasis also should be on making the practices fun and reinforcing, and avoiding a test-like atmosphere. The leader (or other staff members) should closely monitor each role-play and provide feedback to youth on their level of participation and seriousness. The leader should end the role-plays by praising the youth for their efforts and having a discussion about what was practiced.

**Example:**

**Leader:** *"Okay, then, let's review the steps of accepting 'No' for an answer one more time. Then we can practice it together. Whenever someone tells you 'No,' you should keep looking at the person, acknowledge the answer in a calm voice, and not argue or pout. And if you disagree or have a question, bring it up later. Tom, how about you practicing once with me? In this situation, Tom, I'll play the part of your dad and you're going to ask me if you can go out with some friends. When I tell you 'No,' I want you to use all of the behaviors we just described. After we practice, you and Alicia can try a few situations together."*

**The leader and Tom role-play the situation.**

**Leader:** *"Tom, that was great! You kept looking at me the whole time we were talking, said 'Okay, maybe I can go later,' and did not argue or start whining. That's just how to accept 'No' for an answer. Why don't you and Alicia try it?*

*In your situation, Tom can be Alicia's boss, and Alicia can play an employee who is asking to leave work early."*

**Tom and Alicia role-play the situation.**

**Leader:** *"You both did a really super job on this skill. You stayed on task and listened really well. I hope you see how accepting 'No' answers in an appropriate way can help you out in school, on a summer job, and back home with your parents."*

5. **Have youth earn positive consequences (Individual/Group):** At this point, each group member earns a consequence for the amount and quality of his or her participation in the group. The positive consequences that are awarded can be either privilege-based or token-based, or a combination that incorporates the motivation system that is in effect in the program. At the conclusion of the session, a reward, such as a special snack or activity, can be offered to the entire group based on some pre-arranged contingency agreement. The important aspects of the positive consequence component are that the rewards are meaningful and valued by the participants, and are specifically paired with whatever behavior the leader wishes to see again in the future and considers a priority (i.e., participation and effort versus flawless skill performance).

**NOTE:** If the leader wants to teach a second skill, he or she can either save the positive consequences until all of the practices and role-plays are completed or provide a consequence after each skill is practiced individually.

**Example:**

**Leader:** *"Each of you did really well today. Bill and Alicia, you've each earned 500 points for practicing accepting 'No' for an answer and 500 points for listening and participating in our group today. Tom, since accepting 'No' is a*

*special target area for you, you've earned 1,000 points for doing so well at the role-play and 500 points for staying on task in our group. Everyone also worked so hard today that we are going down the street to get some ice cream when we are done here. And when we get back, you all can play video games for 15 minutes."*

6. **Give a generalization assignment and prompt:** In the final component of the group-training format, the leader may give an assignment that the youth are to complete outside the group and report on at the next session. The generalization assignment is a key ingredient in helping the youth learn to use skills in many different situations (Goldstein et al., 1980). The assignments themselves can range from written homework reviews of group topics to journal recordings on the success (or lack thereof) encountered in implementing the target skills. The group is then adjourned with more prompts and encouragement for group members, and an opportunity to use privileges or rewards.

**Example:**

**Leader:** *"Your assignment for our next meeting is to record in your notebooks all the times people tell you 'No' this week and what your response is to them. And if you can, write down what their reaction is when you accept 'No' in a positive way by looking at them, saying 'Okay,' and not arguing. I'll be interested to see how this skill, and all of the skills we talk about here, help you in situations that have caused you problems in the past. If there isn't anything else, we'll adjourn our meeting and go down the street for that ice cream! Thanks, everybody."*

This sample format for a skills-training group is limited only by the creativity of the leader (and other participating adults) and the needs of the youth in the group. Variations in terms of role-play activities, audio-visuals, reinforcers, etc., only serve to enrich the process and make it more enjoyable for the youth. Leaders of social skills groups have ranked boredom and inattentiveness as the primary barriers to their groups' smooth functioning (Howing et al., 1990). Boredom can be addressed by varying teaching methods and materials, as well as the reinforcement available, in order to maintain the youths' interest and enthusiasm.

Inattentiveness is one of many ongoing behaviors that should be closely monitored during the group session and corrected if necessary. Some techniques for addressing the behavior of group participants are discussed next.

# Maintaining a Productive Group Atmosphere

A number of procedures can be used to help maintain a group environment that is enjoyable, yet productive and goal-directed. This is possible only if group members display certain behaviors while participating that are not distracting, disruptive, or apathetic (nonparticipation). However, given that youth usually are referred to a group due to lower-than-expected social skill functioning, group leaders and other involved adults must assume that the positive behaviors necessary for a smooth-running group will occur only with a significant amount of proactive and ongoing teaching. The main purpose of this teaching is to educate group members and prevent disruptive and other inappropriate behaviors during group sessions. Even then, it is quite likely that some youth will become distracted or irritable, or even completely lose emotional control during a group session. Overall, the best approach to use is one that has been thought out and even rehearsed in advance of these problems. That's why it is necessary for group leaders to define which behaviors will be praised, which will be addressed through Corrective Teaching,

and what interventions will occur if a youth must be removed from the group. Consequences for positive and negative behaviors should be planned out in advance as well.

Once group leaders have created a list of expected behaviors (rules and guidelines) and corresponding consequences for group sessions, they can teach these behaviors to each potential group member individually before they meet for the first time. They then can review the behaviors at the group's first session. After that, each meeting can begin with a brief review of the group's rules as a preventive prompt and a reminder to each member of his or her responsibility. Visual prompts such as posters, handouts, and note cards also can serve as effective cues for using appropriate skills. This preventive work is rounded off by reviewing the rewards that are available at the conclusion of the group session for individuals who display attentive behaviors and participate in activities.

The adults who are leading a skills group must closely monitor the youths' behaviors during the group session. As we mentioned earlier, it is a good idea to have two "co-leaders" for each session. Should a youth require individual attention or corrective feedback, one leader can continue with the group while the other works with that youth. The leaders should remember, however, that ongoing praise and reinforcement of positive group behaviors is as equally critical as corrective feedback for negative behaviors. Praise and reinforcement not only helps ensure that youth will continue to use positive behaviors, but also enhances the positive atmosphere within the group. Figure 3 features a partial list of behaviors that should be addressed in a group setting.

In addition to the leaders' ongoing prompting and teaching to youth behaviors, numerous other approaches can be used to maintain productive skills groups with children and adolescents. One technique for intervening in serious peer conflicts is called "fair fighting" (Friedman

## POSITIVE AND NEGATIVE GROUP BEHAVIORS TO ADDRESS

### Behaviors to reinforce

1. Raising hands and waiting to be called on

2. Being attentive and remaining on task

3. Volunteering and participating in activities

4. Making positive comments about others

5. Following directions and accepting feedback

### Behaviors to correct

1. Calling out or leaving seat without permission

2. Distracting others, fidgeting, or yawning

3. Making negative comments or insulting others

4. Bragging about inappropriate behavior

5. Noncompliance, arguing, and complaining

*Figure 3*

et al., 1983). In this technique, when two youth become extremely angry at each other, they are initially separated and each one goes to a private area to talk to an adult alone. Each youth tells his or her side of the argument to the adult, who gives the youth instructions to calm down. The youth and the two adults then get together, and the youth observe the adults discuss the problem issue from the youths' perspective and arrive at a resolution. This serves to defuse the immediate crisis situation and allows adults to model appropriate conflict resolution strategies for the youth.

# Summary

Teaching skills in group settings can be a viable alternative for many children and youth who require instruction in interpersonal skills.

The group setting functions almost like a "sheltered workshop" for socially deficient youth where they can learn, practice, and generalize skills that will be critical to their success in almost every arena of life. Group teaching also can function effectively as an additional treatment strategy for each youth individually. A youth's specific needs are best addressed through a comprehensive, integrated treatment approach that prepares the youth for less-restrictive living or educational alternatives, and improves his or her overall social functioning.

One hallmark of the Boys Town Teaching Model is a system called "Self-Government," which is designed to encourage group participation and decision-making. One component of the Self-Government System is a nightly meeting of the youth and their caregivers called "Family Meeting." Within the structure of this meeting, each youth has an opportunity to discuss problems, offer potential solutions, and even vote on certain house rules. The caregivers use this nightly meeting to encourage group problem-solving, give each youth a chance to provide input about the operation of the program, and teach a wide variety of important social skills (discussion skills, giving and receiving criticism, reporting problems, etc.). In this way, each youth's individual Treatment Plan is augmented by what is taught and reinforced during Family Meeting.

# CHAPTER 6

# Social Skills and Treatment Planning

Children and adolescents, like all human beings, are part of social groups. They depend on relationships with others to meet even their most basic needs. A child's sense of well-being is directly related to his or her success, or lack of success, in dealing with significant others.

Early in life, young people learn that there are consequences, both positive and negative, attached to how they interact with others and how they choose to respond in social situations. This process of "socialization" begins in the earliest interactions between infant and parent; it prepares kids for more difficult situations later in childhood and through the teenage years. Ideally, lessons learned at each stage in a child's development become the tools he or she uses to successfully meet the challenges presented at later stages of life.

Today, young people face an increasingly difficult world. Many factors can affect a child's ability to learn new skills and change behaviors. Age, developmental level, family problems, substance abuse, economic pressures, the lure of gangs, delinquency, and many other external issues threaten children physically, emotionally, and spiritually. Also, internal issues like possible chemical imbalances in a child's brain, genetic traits inherited from a child's parents, medical problems, and others can have an impact on learning and behavior. In addition, a child's thoughts and feelings – the way a child looks at the world – have been shaped by his or her past experiences, and play a major role in how a young person interacts with others.

During the past two decades, a convincing body of evidence indicates that unless children achieve minimal social competence by about age 6, they have a high probability of being at risk into adulthood in several ways (Ladd, 2000; Parker & Asher, 1987). Recent research (Hartup & Moore, 1990; Kinsey, 2000; Ladd & Profilet, 1996; McClellan & Kinsey, 1999; Parker & Asher, 1987; Rogoff, 1990) suggests that a child's long-term social and emotional adaptation, academic and cognitive development, and citizenship are enhanced by frequent opportunities to strengthen social competence during childhood. All of these factors must be considered when developing effective treatment for youth.

In order to successfully cope with these external and internal issues, young people must learn how to interact with others in socially acceptable ways and make appropriate decisions in social situations. In treatment settings, this means developing an individual treatment plan for each youth that identifies the youth's needs, strengths, and deficiencies, and incorporates social skill instruction (along with other interventions) to address these areas. This chapter focuses on the reasons children need treatment and the role of teaching social skills in treatment planning.

# Why Kids Misbehave

Youth require intervention and treatment for many reasons. At Boys Town, we have determined that one of the most influential factors in the development of behavioral and/or mental health problems is that youth have not yet learned the social skills needed to overcome the problems in their lives. In most cases, when troubled youth require treatment, the environments they come from have significantly contributed to and fostered the formation of problem behaviors and/or mental health difficulties

A number of factors contained within the home, community, and school are related to antisocial behavior (Mayer, 2001). However, a factor that cuts across all three of these areas is an aversive or punitive environment (De-Baryshe, Patterson, & Capaldi, 1993; Dishion, 1992; Elliott, 1992; Mayer, 1995). Research has taught us that aversive or punitive environments predictably promote antisocial behaviors such as aggression, violence, vandalism, and escape (Azrin, Hake, Holz, & Hutchinson, 1965; Berkowitz, 1983; Mayer, 1995). However, these learned inappropriate behaviors and skills serve a purpose: They enable the youth to get what he or she needs and wants.

Over time, these same behaviors and skills become reinforced and strengthened, and eventually spill over to other environments (e.g., school, sports teams, jobs, relationships with peers and adults, and so on). In these new settings, youth try to use the same negative behaviors that were "successful" for them in the past. But when they don't work, kids flounder, not knowing what it takes to be successful. So, in order for youth to succeed in previous and new environments, situations, and relationships, they must learn new prosocial skills that will help them to get their needs met in ways that are more socially acceptable.

With social skill instruction, youth learn skills that are determined to be the most func-

tional for them and will produce the best long-term results. This means that every youth requires individual treatment. Some youngsters will initially need to learn the most basic skills (e.g., "Following Instructions," "Accepting Consequences," "Accepting 'No' for an Answer," etc.) so that a foundation can be laid for learning more complex skills (e.g., "Expressing Feelings Appropriately," "Resisting Peer Pressure," "Spontaneous Problem-Solving," etc.). Many times, caregivers and other adults will need to gradually shape a youth's behavior by patiently teaching basic social skills so that the youth can learn the final desired behavior. This can be a slow, arduous process for caregivers and youth, but it is necessary if the youth is to overcome his or her problems.

The use of appropriate social skills involves an immensely complex chain of rapidly occurring interpersonal events. For youth, especially those suffering from behavioral and mental health disorders that dramatically limit their emotional and cognitive functioning, correctly performing these skills at the right time can be an overwhelming task. They have considerable difficulty organizing and blending their behaviors into smooth-flowing interactions with others, particularly under stressful conditions. So, supervisors in treatment or care settings should encourage caregivers to adjust their teaching techniques, vocabulary, and interpersonal behaviors to best meet the learning style of each youth.

When assigning social skills for treatment, it is important for a caregiver or treatment team (i.e., supervisors, caregivers, and other adults involved with the youth) to take into account individual factors like the age and developmental level of the youth, the severity of the youth's behaviors, the length of time a youth has been exposed to social skill instruction, and so on. These factors play a pivotal role in the success or failure of each youth's treatment plan. Once the most appropriate skills have been identified and prioritized, caregivers can use various teaching interactions to reinforce and teach youth new prosocial ways of getting their needs met. (At Boys Town, these interactions include Proactive Teaching, Effective Praise, and Corrective Teaching. See Chapter 3.) It also is critical to identify and target the specific situations and antecedent conditions in which the problem behavior occurs. (See Chapter 2.)

Culture and background also greatly influence behaviors, appearance, expression of affect or feelings, thoughts and cognitions, and language. Because all behavior is culture-based, social behaviors need to be defined and interpreted in a cultural context. Culture is not inherited but learned, passed on over generations and transmitted largely through the institutions of family and school. Parenting practices and family dynamics greatly influence a child's beliefs, values, social attitudes, and eventual behavioral patterns that are reflective of these teachings (Cartledge & Milburn, 1996).

As we've said, one part of successful treatment planning is to identify and target appropriate social skills. Thus, a treatment team must consider a child's culture and the critical role it plays in his or her behaviors, thoughts, and perceptions. For example, looking at an adult is the first step in almost all of the social skills that kids are taught at Boys Town. However, this behavior may be a sign of disrespect or defiance for children in some cultures. Knowing that a child of a specific culture holds such a belief directly affects how one teaches social skills to that child. Skill steps may have to be modified to meet the child's needs and the child may have to learn to determine whether or not to use all of the steps of a skill in different situations.

# Treatment Planning for Youth Problems and Behaviors

The appropriate choice of skills to teach youth is critical to the teaching process and the eventual success of the learner. This is true for all youth behaviors, but it's especially true when a caregiver or treatment team is confronted with particularly difficult or troublesome behaviors from their youth. Boys Town's working definition of "difficult" youth problems includes those behaviors that can cause harm to the youth and others, that persist chronically over time, and that may eventually lead to negative program departure and other negative consequences for the youth. This definition includes behaviors such as stealing, physical aggression, chronic noncompliance, running away, truancy, sexual acting out and sexual aggression, and drug use – all of which necessitate a systematic approach to treatment planning and target skill selection.

In general terms, the treatment team decides what skills to target for "typical" youth problems or treatment issues by first analyzing the functional relationships that exist in the youth's environment that appear to reinforce the problem behaviors. It also is critical that the specific situations and antecedent conditions in which the behaviors occur be identified and targeted. Caregivers then can begin preventive measures through Proactive Teaching, and systematically begin to teach appropriate alternative response sets (i.e., the individual skills listed in the Social Skills Curriculum). The treatment team must be sure, however, that the targeted skills directly address the problem behavior and occur under the same situational variables that are associated with the problem behavior being treated.

Oftentimes, a youth may have many negative behaviors and skill deficits, or have particularly serious behavior problems. In the area of identifying which social skills to teach and how to teach them, a systematic analysis of a youth's problem behaviors and the contingencies that appear to be supporting them is necessary when developing or revising a treatment plan. A process used at Boys Town for formulating a "specialized" treatment plan for difficult youth problems is summarized in Figure 1. An explanation of each step in the process follows. This process can be adapted by programs that develop or wish to develop treatment plans for their youth.

---

### TREATMENT PLANNING PROCESS

1. Problem inventory
2. Problem selection
3. Problem specification
4. Baselining
5. Specification of treatment goals
6. Formulation of treatment strategies
7. Follow-up/Revision
8. Maintenance

*Figure 1*

---

1. **Problem inventory.** The treatment team begins by generating a list of all relevant problem behaviors the youth is displaying. This is a brainstorming session designed to inventory all of the youth's behavioral deficits currently being observed by team members (i.e., caregivers, teachers at school, coaches, program supervisors, therapists, parents, etc.). The problem behaviors need not be listed in any particular order or priority, but as they are mentioned by team members who are involved directly with the youth. The process of prioritization begins later. This step also gives caregivers a chance to discuss any frustrations they are having in working with the youth and to deal with any negative emotions they may be experiencing.

2. **Problem selection.** In this step, the treatment team begins to discuss and then decide what behaviors listed in the youth's problem inventory appear to be of the greatest immediate concern. Supervisors or therapists (or

whoever takes the lead) assist this decision-making process by prompting discussion on issues such as: 1) What problem behavior occurs most often?; 2) What behavior relates most closely to several other behaviors that were listed?; 3) What behavior causes the most trouble or failure for the youth?; 4) What behavior presents the greatest danger to others?; and 5) What behavior causes the most distress to the adults, family members, or peers who interact with the youth? In this step, the treatment team should prioritize the problem behaviors that were generated and select the primary behavioral issues to be addressed first. The final choice of what problem behaviors to focus on should also be left to the primary caregiver or those who work closely with the youth. Problems can be made worse when team members differ widely on what behaviors are the most disruptive or difficult to address. Behaviors can be treated most effectively when all treatment team members consistently respond to targeted problem behaviors in a well-defined manner.

3. **Problem specification.** In this step, the problem behaviors the treatment team has chosen to address are clearly defined and specified. This is necessary in order to facilitate more effective treatment by the primary caregivers and quicker learning of alternative behaviors by the youth. First, the actual circumstances in which the problem behaviors consistently occur are noted, as well as other variables such as time of day, location, and people who usually are present when the behaviors occur. It also is important to note the social or verbal interactions (antecedents) that take place immediately before the youth engages in the inappropriate behaviors. These factors help determine the social skill areas in which teaching will take place with the youth.

In addition, the team specifies the youth's actual verbal and physical problem behaviors. Whether the youth's voice becomes elevated or sullen, or whether his or her verbal statements are sarcastic or threatening are important in defining appropriate responses. When problem behaviors are clearly defined, the treatment team is able to more easily identify the appropriate alternative responses to teach. In addition to specifying the youth's problem behaviors, the treatment team should list the typical consequences that have followed the inappropriate behavior. This would include the consequences that caregivers have used (e.g., restricting privileges, tokens/points, chores, etc.) in the past when trying to treat the problem, as well as social responses of others (e.g., attention, ignoring, getting upset) who have been present when the youth displayed the inappropriate behaviors. This analysis can increase the treatment team's insights into what contingencies have been supporting the youth's problematic responses.

The problem specification step ends when the team has identified the alternative skills – or "target skills" – to teach the youth in the same situations or circumstances that the problem behaviors previously occurred. The target skills should be "functional" in that they empower the youth to appropriately handle the situations that have caused the most problems. The emphasis should be on choosing skills that eventually will be reinforcing to the youth and help him or her meet treatment goals and needs in a socially acceptable manner.

4. **Baselining.** It is critical for the team to have some knowledge of how often a youth's target behaviors occur. By recording these behaviors daily, weekly, or monthly, caregivers can measure the effectiveness of their teaching over time. A "baseline" measurement is the frequency of a particular behavior's occurrence prior to introducing a new intervention. This measurement can be obtained in formal and informal ways (e.g., charting, frequency count, estimating, data collection, moving a penny from one pocket to the other when behavior occurs, etc.). The treatment team can derive a formal baseline measurement from systematic observation of the youth in various circumstances, and from carefully recorded clinical/treatment documentation.

An informal baseline measurement can be based on the caregivers' recall of when, where, how often, and under what circumstances a behavior occurs. The goal is to obtain the most accurate measure possible to use as a comparison after the teaching strategy has been in place for a period of time. The treatment team also should estimate how often the youth may use the appropriate replacement skill. This will help the team evaluate whether the caregivers' teaching is increasing the youth's use of the skill while decreasing the negative behavior that was targeted.

5. **Specification of treatment goals.** At this point in the treatment planning process for social skill instruction, the treatment team must decide, given the current level of the youth's functioning, what percent of the time they would initially like to see the youth use the target skill. For example, the baselining step reveals that a particular youth correctly follows the caregivers' instructions only two out of every 10 times, and refuses to follow instructions the other eight times. Caregivers might then plan to teach the skill of "Following Instructions" to the youth for the first two weeks of treatment with the goal of having him improve to five out of 10 times. Eventually, the goal should be increased to 90 percent, or even 100 percent. Remember, however, that it is important for both the youth and

the treatment team that initial skill goals are reasonable and obtainable.

Goal specification also should be related to the components of the particular skill being taught. For example, the eventual goal of teaching a youth to follow instructions would be to have the youth use all of the skill's component behaviors (i.e., look at the person, say "Okay," do the task, and check back) when directed to engage in an activity by caregivers, teachers at school, parents, and others. By specifying the behaviors to be used in "instruction" situations, caregivers are more likely to be consistent in their expectations and teaching, which enables the youth to be more successful in meeting those expectations and being rewarded for doing so.

6. **Formulation of treatment strategies.**
In this step, the treatment team agrees on what strategies will be used and integrated in the teaching of the target skill. These strategies may include preventive skill-building exercises and role-play (Proactive Teaching), spontaneous efforts to reinforce positive performance in the skill area (Effective Praise), recognition of negative performance and alternative skill-teaching (Corrective Teaching), and consistent use of rewards and privilege losses that are contingent on the youth's behavior. Other techniques such as participation in a social skills group, practice with parents or peers, and counseling interventions may be integrated into this plan as well. Also included are efforts to promote the youth's generalization of the target skill to other situations and environments where the skill may be used. Since using the target skill in other diverse situations is a key indicator that the youth is learning, caregivers should monitor this area to measure progress.

In applying the various teaching strategies, it is important that the caregivers are clear

on such issues as how each technique is to be used and applied, when and how often each strategy will be used, and in what situations the caregivers will use each technique. Again, consistency among the adults working with and caring for the youth is critical.

The treatment team also should develop a monitoring or data collection system to track the youth's performance of the targeted social skill. The emphasis here is to collect sufficient information on the effectiveness of the teaching strategies so that successful techniques can continue and less-productive techniques can be revised.

7. **Follow-up/Revision.** After implementing the skill-based treatment plan, the treatment team meets to review the treatment goals that were set for the youth and the progress that has been made. The team compares the youth's current level of functioning in the targeted skill area with the baseline data collected earlier. If there are negative data trends (i.e., the youth has made no progress or demonstrates the skill less frequently than before), the treatment team should review the plan. There may be problems in the way it is being implemented by the caregivers that can be corrected with further training or by further specifying the strategies. Oftentimes, caregivers, parents, teachers, and other adults need a lot of encouragement and support to respond differently to a youth's behavior. Also, it is important that the person who is directing the intervention consistently monitors the caregivers' social skill instruction to ensure that they are focused on and effectively teaching to targeted social skills.

If it appears the plan has been implemented correctly and has been used long enough to be effective, but there still is no progress, the treatment team can revise specific aspects of the treatment plan. This could involve changing the frequency of Proactive Teaching and cued practice exercises, revising the consequences that are being offered, or even changing the skill itself. The important part of this process is making such decisions based on concerted observation of the youth's skills and any data that can be collected.

If the data on the youth's learning of the targeted social skill indicates a positive trend (i.e., the youth is meeting improvement goals and showing a degree of generalization), the treatment team may decide to continue to use the current treatment plan. The team could, however, set a higher goal for performance of the skill, such as having the youth follow instructions nine or 10 out of 10 times instructions are given to him or her by caregivers, teachers at school, etc. When the goals for this level of performance are consistently being met, the team can decide to move on to the last step of the treatment planning process and focus treatment efforts on other prioritized skill deficits.

8. **Maintenance.** We know that a youth will not consistently continue to use a newly learned skill without intermittent reinforcement. In this step, the treatment team devises a specific plan for maintaining and reinforcing the youth's progress. Formal Proactive Teaching and practice sessions can be gradually decreased to only once per week or month, instead of daily as in the original plan, and the use of artificial rewards such as earned tokens/points and privileges may be gradually removed. It is critical during this fading process that the social reinforcement of the youth's use of targeted skills be consistent and frequent. In other words, when the youth demonstrates a positive skill that now no longer earns him or her tangible positive consequences or privileges, the caregivers still should respond with enthusiastic and meaningful praise. Effective Praise

should still be used, but without a tangible reward in the consequence step. Follow-up on the youth's progress should be ongoing and revised as needed. If a youth regresses to an earlier level of skill use, the original plan (or modifications of the plan) can be reinstated.

# Additional Assistance in Treatment Planning

As an additional aid to the treatment planning process, Appendix C of this manual offers a listing of Curriculum skills grouped by behavior problems and Appendix D lists skills by situations. Appendix C provides a quick reference for caregivers who need to identify skills that can be used in the treatment of a youth who is demonstrating behaviors that are characteristic of a particular problem area (e.g., aggressive and antisocial behavior, depression and withdrawal, etc.). The skills listed under a particular problem behavior are those that may positively affect the youth's functioning in that area. Appendix D lists several common situations or circumstances a young person may encounter. The skills listed under each situation are ones that may assist the youth in appropriately responding to the demands of that situation.

In both cases, the decision on which skills are appropriate to teach a particular youth must be based on a functional assessment of a particular youth's needs and abilities. Thus, the listings provided in Appendix C and D are not intended as a "cookbook" for planning the treatment of a young person, but rather as a guide for caregivers in selecting relevant skills to teach the youth.

Another helpful resource is Boys Town's book, *Treating Youth with DSM-IV Disorders: The Role of Social Skill Instruction.* This book contains a series of charts that list social skills to teach to children and adolescents who require treatment for specific DSM-IV disorders.

# Summary

Treatment planning charts the course for a youth's improvement in the way he or she thinks, feels, and behaves. Effective treatment planning considers the many factors that contributed to a youth's present state, the youth's strengths and weaknesses, and the best ways to change negative behaviors and reinforce positive ones. A good treatment planning process is individualized, positive, and focused on teaching the appropriate social skills, and empowers youth to make good decisions. It also emphasizes the long-term goals of helping youth internalize and generalize social skills.

# CHAPTER 7
# The Social Skills Curriculum

The 182 skills of the Boys Town Social Skills Curriculum are drawn from the vast number of situational variables young people might encounter as they grow and develop toward independence. Each skill has been task-analyzed into its essential behavioral elements that may include: 1) specific verbal responses; 2) nonverbal behaviors; 3) specific behaviors to omit; 4) behavioral cues and self-instructions; and, in some cases, 5) subclasses of skills that may be learned separately. The focus here is to provide caregivers and treatment teams with a comprehensive resource they can use when developing effective, therapeutic treatment plans. (Treatment teams can consist of anyone involved in a child's care – parents, therapists, direct-care staff, supervisors, teachers, school principals, counselors, etc. These teams would have the most immediate and consistent means of implementing the treatment plan.)

The skills in the Curriculum are organized into four groups – **Basic, Intermediate, Advanced,** and **Complex** – according to the perceived complexity associated with the performance of each skill. The degree of difficulty increases from Group 1 (Basic Skills) to Group 4 (Complex Skills), mainly due to the number of component behaviors required to perform the more advanced or complex skills or because of the difficulties of situations associated with those skills.

The nature of many of the component behaviors of the listed skills also changes with increasing complexity. Skills found in the more complex groupings of the Curriculum will be more likely to contain cognitive or "metabehavioral" steps. Examples of these include cues to a youth to identify characteristics of the immediate situation, notice the responses of other people involved, monitor his or her own responses and feelings, and instruct himself or herself to engage in certain activities. This added area of learning, along with the specific behavioral responses previously taught by the caretaker, greatly increases the youth's repertoire of skills that can be drawn from in complex, and demanding, situations.

The Social Skills Curriculum is structured so that the last group is likely to include skills that have many more of these cognitive-based component steps, whereas the first group could be considered more "basic" behavioral skills. Many youth in treatment programs typically begin learning the basic social skills first, and then advance to the more complex skill areas contained in the higher levels. But this may not always be the case. The idea is not that all youth need to learn the skills from each group in the precise order in which they are categorized, but rather that skills can be chosen from the Curriculum that match each youth's individual behavioral needs, abilities, and treatment issues. The system of groups simply gives the child-care staff or teacher some measure of relative complexity when prioritizing skills for a youth.

Likewise, when organizing the Curriculum for a social skills training group, instructors would require some measure of cognitive involvement and difficulty in order to appropriately match the Curriculum content to the abilities of the participants. The appropriate choice of skills to teach a youth or group is critical to the teaching process and the eventual success of the learner. This is especially true when staff members are confronted with particularly difficult or troublesome behaviors from their youth.

In the remainder of this chapter, we list the 182 skills of the Social Skills Curriculum, numbered and grouped according to their degree of complexity. Following the list is a large section where all of the skills are presented with their respective steps. In that section, rationales and helpful hints are offered for each of the eight Basic Skills.

---

For schoolteachers and others who provide instruction in educational settings, Boys Town offers the book, *Tools for Teaching Social Skills in School*. This book provides lesson plans for teaching specific skills, reproducible skill pages, techniques and examples for blending skill-teaching with academic lessons, ideas for motivating and monitoring behavior, and strategies for increasing parent support and involvement. *Tools for Teaching Social Skills in School* is available through the Boys Town Press.

---

# Basic Skills Group

| Skill 1 | Following Instructions |
|---|---|
| Skill 2 | Accepting "No" for an Answer |
| Skill 3 | Talking with Others |
| Skill 4 | Introducing Yourself |
| Skill 5 | Accepting Criticism or a Consequence |
| Skill 6 | Disagreeing Appropriately |
| Skill 7 | Showing Respect |
| Skill 8 | Showing Sensitivity to Others |

# Intermediate Skills Group

| Skill 9 | Accepting Apologies from Others |
|---|---|

| Skill 10 | Accepting Compliments |
|---|---|
| Skill 11 | Accepting Consequences |
| Skill 12 | Accepting Decisions of Authority |
| Skill 13 | Answering the Telephone |
| Skill 14 | Asking for Clarification |
| Skill 15 | Asking for Help |
| Skill 16 | Asking Questions |
| Skill 17 | Being on Time (Promptness) |
| Skill 18 | Checking In (or Checking Back) |
| Skill 19 | Choosing Appropriate Words to Say |
| Skill 20 | Closing a Conversation |
| Skill 21 | Completing Homework |
| Skill 22 | Completing Tasks |
| Skill 23 | Complying with Reasonable Requests |
| Skill 24 | Contributing to Discussions (Joining in a Conversation) |
| Skill 25 | Correcting Another Person (or Giving Criticism) |
| Skill 26 | Doing Good Quality Work |
| Skill 27 | Following Rules |
| Skill 28 | Following Written Instructions |
| Skill 29 | Getting Another Person's Attention |
| Skill 30 | Getting the Teacher's Attention |
| Skill 31 | Giving Compliments |
| Skill 32 | Greeting Others |
| Skill 33 | Ignoring Distractions by Others |
| Skill 34 | Initiating a Conversation |
| Skill 35 | Interrupting Appropriately |
| Skill 36 | Introducing Others |
| Skill 37 | Listening to Others |
| Skill 38 | Maintaining a Conversation |
| Skill 39 | Maintaining an Appropriate Appearance |
| Skill 40 | Maintaining Personal Hygiene |
| Skill 41 | Making an Apology |
| Skill 42 | Making a Request (Asking a Favor) |
| Skill 43 | Making a Telephone Call |
| Skill 44 | Making Positive Self-Statements |

Skill 45   Making Positive Statements about Others
Skill 46   Offering Assistance or Help
Skill 47   Participating in Activities
Skill 48   Refraining from Possessing Contraband or Drugs
Skill 49   Reporting Emergencies
Skill 50   Reporting Other Youths' Behavior (or Peer Reporting)
Skill 51   Resisting Peer Pressure
Skill 52   Saying Good-Bye to Guests
Skill 53   Saying "No" Assertively
Skill 54   Seeking Positive Attention
Skill 55   Showing Appreciation
Skill 56   Showing Interest
Skill 57   Staying on Task
Skill 58   Trying New Tasks
Skill 59   Using an Appropriate Voice Tone
Skill 60   Using Anger Control Strategies
Skill 61   Using Structured Problem-Solving (SODAS)
Skill 62   Using Table Etiquette
Skill 63   Volunteering
Skill 64   Waiting Your Turn

## Advanced Skills Group

Skill 65   Accepting Defeat or Loss
Skill 66   Accepting Help or Assistance
Skill 67   Accepting Winning Appropriately
Skill 68   Advocating for Oneself
Skill 69   Analyzing Skills Needed for Different Situations
Skill 70   Analyzing Social Situations
Skill 71   Analyzing Tasks to Be Completed
Skill 72   Being Prepared for Class
Skill 73   Borrowing from Others
Skill 74   Caring for Others' Property
Skill 75   Caring for Own Belongings

Skill 76   Choosing Appropriate Clothing
Skill 77   Choosing Appropriate Friends
Skill 78   Communicating Honestly
Skill 79   Complying with School Dress Code
Skill 80   Compromising with Others
Skill 81   Concentrating on a Subject or Task
Skill 82   Contributing to Group Activities
Skill 83   Controlling Eating Habits
Skill 84   Controlling Emotions
Skill 85   Controlling Sexually Abusive Impulses toward Others
Skill 86   Controlling the Impulse to Lie
Skill 87   Controlling the Impulse to Steal
Skill 88   Cooperating with Others
Skill 89   Coping with Anger and Aggression from Others
Skill 90   Coping with Change
Skill 91   Coping with Conflict
Skill 92   Coping with Sad Feelings (or Depression)
Skill 93   Dealing with an Accusation
Skill 94   Dealing with Being Left Out
Skill 95   Dealing with Boredom
Skill 96   Dealing with Contradictory Messages
Skill 97   Dealing with Embarrassing Situations
Skill 98   Dealing with Failure
Skill 99   Dealing with Fear
Skill 100  Dealing with Frustration
Skill 101  Dealing with Group Pressure
Skill 102  Dealing with Rejection
Skill 103  Delaying Gratification
Skill 104  Displaying Effort
Skill 105  Displaying Sportsmanship
Skill 106  Expressing Appropriate Affection
Skill 107  Expressing Feelings Appropriately
Skill 108  Expressing Optimism
Skill 109  Expressing Pride in Accomplishments

Skill 110   Following Safety Rules

Skill 111   Following Through on Agreements and Contracts

Skill 112   Giving Instructions

Skill 113   Giving Rationales

Skill 114   Interacting Appropriately with Members of the Opposite Sex

Skill 115   Keeping Property in Its Place

Skill 116   Lending to Others

Skill 117   Making Decisions

Skill 118   Making New Friends

Skill 119   Making Restitution (Compensating)

Skill 120   Managing Time

Skill 121   Negotiating with Others

Skill 122   Organizing Tasks and Activities

Skill 123   Persevering on Tasks and Projects

Skill 124   Planning Meals

Skill 125   Preparing for a Stressful Conversation

Skill 126   Preventing Trouble with Others

Skill 127   Problem-Solving a Disagreement

Skill 128   Responding to Complaints

Skill 129   Responding to Others' Feelings

Skill 130   Responding to Others' Humor

Skill 131   Responding to Teasing

Skill 132   Responding to Written Requests

Skill 133   Self-Correcting Own Behavior

Skill 134   Self-Reporting Own Behaviors

Skill 135   Setting Appropriate Boundaries

Skill 136   Sharing Attention with Others

Skill 137   Sharing Personal Experiences

Skill 138   Suggesting an Activity

Skill 139   Using Appropriate Humor

Skill 140   Using Appropriate Language

Skill 141   Using Relaxation Strategies

Skill 142   Using Self-Talk or Self-Instruction

Skill 143   Using Spontaneous Problem-Solving

Skill 144   Using Study Skills

Skill 145   Working Independently

# Complex Skills Group

Skill 146   Accepting Self

Skill 147   Altering One's Environment

Skill 148   Asking for Advice

Skill 149   Assessing Own Abilities

Skill 150   Being an Appropriate Role Model

Skill 151   Being a Consumer

Skill 152   Being Assertive

Skill 153   Being Patient

Skill 154   Budgeting and Managing Money

Skill 155   Clarifying Values and Beliefs

Skill 156   Differentiating Friends from Acquaintances

Skill 157   Displaying Appropriate Control

Skill 158   Expressing Empathy and Understanding for Others

Skill 159   Expressing Grief

Skill 160   Formulating Strategies

Skill 161   Gathering Information

Skill 162   Identifying Own Feelings

Skill 163   Interviewing for a Job

Skill 164   Laughing at Oneself

Skill 165   Maintaining Relationships

Skill 166   Making an Appropriate Complaint

Skill 167   Making Moral and Spiritual Decisions

Skill 168   Managing Stress

Skill 169   Planning Ahead

Skill 170   Recognizing Moods of Others

Skill 171   Resigning from a Job or Project

Skill 172   Resolving Conflicts

Skill 173   Rewarding Yourself

Skill 174   Seeking Professional Assistance

Skill 175   Setting Goals

Skill 176   Stopping Negative or Harmful Thoughts

Skill 177   Taking Risks Appropriately

Skill 178   Tolerating Differences

Skill 179   Using Community Resources

Skill 180   Using Leisure Time

Skill 181   Using Self-Monitoring and Self-Reflection

Skill 182   Using Strategies to Find a Job

# Basic Skills

## 1. Following instructions

1. Look at the person.
2. Say "Okay."
3. Do what you've been asked right away.
4. Check back.

## 2. Accepting "No" for an answer

1. Look at the person.
2. Say "Okay."
3. Stay calm.
4. If you disagree, ask later.

## 3. Talking with others

1. Look at the person.
2. Use a pleasant voice.
3. Ask questions.
4. Don't interrupt.

## 4. Introducing yourself

1. Look at the person. Smile.
2. Use a pleasant voice.
3. Offer a greeting. Say "Hi, my name is...."
4. Shake the person's hand.
5. When you leave, say "It was nice to meet you."

## 5. Accepting criticism or a consequence

1. Look at the person.
2. Say "Okay."
3. Don't argue.

## 6. Disagreeing appropriately

1. Look at the person.
2. Use a pleasant voice.
3. Say "I understand how you feel."
4. Tell why you feel differently.
5. Give a reason.
6. Listen to the other person.

## 7. Showing respect

1. Obey a request to stop a negative behavior.
2. Refrain from teasing, threatening, or making fun of others.
3. Allow others to have their privacy.
4. Obtain permission before using another person's property.
5. Do not damage or vandalize public property.
6. Refrain from conning or persuading others into breaking rules.
7. Avoid acting obnoxiously in public.
8. Dress appropriately when in public.

## 8. Showing sensitivity to others

1. Express interest and concern for others, especially when they are having troubles.
2. Recognize that disabled people deserve the same respect as anyone else.
3. Apologize or make amends for hurting someone's feelings or causing harm.
4. Recognize that people of different races, religions, and backgrounds deserve to be treated the same way as you would expect to be treated.

# Following instructions

## 1. Look at the person.

### Rationale:

Looking at the person shows that you are paying attention.

### Helpful hints:

- Look at the person as you would a friend.
- Don't stare, make faces, or roll your eyes.
- Look at the person throughout your conversation.
- Avoid being distracted.
- Looking at the person will help you understand his or her mood.

## 2. Say "Okay."

### Rationale:

Saying "Okay" lets the person know you understand.

### Helpful hints:

- Answer right away.
- Use a pleasant voice.
- Speak clearly.
- Smile and nod your head (if it is appropriate to do so).

## 3. Do what you've been asked right away.

### Rationale:

You are more likely to remember exactly what you're supposed to do if you do it right away.

**Helpful hints:**

- Complete each step of the task.
- Stay on task. Don't let other things interfere.
- Do the best job you can.
- If you have problems, ask for help.

 ## Check back.

### Rationale:

Checking back lets the person know that you have followed the instruction.

### Helpful hints:

- Tell the person you have finished as soon as you are done.
- Explain exactly what you did.
- Ask if the job was done correctly.
- Correct anything that needs to be done over.

## BASIC – SKILL 2
# Accepting "No" for an answer

### 1. Look at the person.

**Rationale:**

Looking at the person shows that you are paying attention.

**Helpful hints:**

- Don't stare or make faces.
- Don't look away.
- If you are upset, control your emotions. Try to relax and stay calm.
- Listening carefully will help you understand what the other person is saying.

### 2. Say "Okay."

**Rationale:**

Saying "Okay" lets the other person know that you understand.

**Helpful hints:**

- Answer right away.
- Speak clearly. Don't mumble.
- Don't sound angry or start to argue. That might lead to problems.
- Take a deep breath if you feel upset.

### 3. Stay calm.

**Rationale:**

Staying calm allows you to hear exactly what the other person is saying.

## Helpful hints:

- If you react negatively, you may make the situation worse.
- People will think you are serious about improving if you stay calm.
- Staying calm shows that you have control of your emotions.
- Accepting a "No" answer this time may improve the chances of getting a "Yes" answer later on.

# 4. If you disagree, ask later.

## Rationale:

If you disagree right away, you will appear to be arguing.

## Helpful hints:

- Take some time to plan how you are going to approach the person who told you "No."
- Plan in advance what you are going to say.
- Accept the answer, even if it is still "No."
- Be sure to thank the person for listening.

## BASIC – SKILL 3
# Talking with others

## 1. Look at the person.

**Rationale:**

Looking at the person shows that you are paying attention and shows the person that you want to talk.

**Helpful hints:**

- Look at the person as you would a friend.
- Look at the person's face; this will help you understand his or her mood.

## 2. Use a pleasant voice.

**Rationale:**

People won't want to talk to someone who seems unpleasant, angry, or threatening.

**Helpful hints:**

- Speak clearly.
- Use short sentences that are easily understood.
- Think before you speak.

## 3. Ask questions.

**Rationale:**

Asking questions includes the other person in the conversation.

**Helpful hints:**

- Avoid asking questions that can be answered with only a "Yes" or a "No."
- Ask the person about his or her opinions, likes and dislikes, and interests.
- Listen intently.
- Be prepared to answer questions the person might ask you.

# 4. Don't interrupt.

### Rationale:

Interrupting shows you don't care what the other person is saying.

### Helpful hints:

- Make sure the person is done speaking before you respond.
- Maintain eye contact.
- Maintain good posture; don't distract the other person by fidgeting.
- Don't monopolize the conversation or jump from topic to topic.

## BASIC – SKILL 4
# Introducing yourself

---

## 1. Look at the person. Smile.

### Rationale:

Looking at the person is one way of showing that you really want to meet him or her.

### Helpful hints:

- Get the person's attention appropriately.
- Don't stare or make faces.
- Look at the person as you would a friend.
- Looking at the person sets a friendly tone for the beginning of your conversation.

## 2. Use a pleasant voice.

### Rationale:

You will make a good impression if you appear to be friendly.

### Helpful hints:

- Speak clearly.
- Talk loud enough to be heard, but not too loud.
- Use proper grammar and avoid slang words.
- Don't interrupt.

## 3. Offer a greeting. Say "Hi, my name is...."

### Rationale:

Saying "Hi" shows you are friendly and makes the other person feel welcome.

### Helpful hints:

- Make sure the person hears you.
- Listen if the other person says anything in return.
- Smile if it is appropriate to do so.

## Shake the person's hand.

### Rationale:

Shaking hands is a traditional way of greeting someone.

### Helpful hints:

- Make sure your hand is clean before shaking hands with someone.
- Use a firm grip, but don't squeeze too hard.
- Three shakes is about right when shaking hands.
- Say "It's nice to meet you" as you shake hands.

## When you leave, say "It was nice to meet you."

### Rationale:

Saying something nice ends your conversation on a friendly note.

### Helpful hints:

- Be sincere.
- Use the person's name again when saying good-bye.
- Remember the person's name should you meet again.

# Accepting criticism or a consequence

## 1. Look at the person.

**Rationale:**

Looking at the person shows that you are paying attention.

**Helpful hints:**

- Don't stare or make faces.
- Look at the person throughout the conversation. Don't look away.
- Listen carefully and try not to be distracted.
- Paying attention shows courtesy; looking away shows disinterest.

## 2. Say "Okay."

**Rationale:**

Saying "Okay" shows that you understand what the other person is saying.

**Helpful hints:**

- Nodding your head also shows that you understand.
- Don't mumble.
- By nodding your head or saying "Okay" frequently throughout a long conversation, you let the speaker know that you are still listening carefully.
- Use a pleasant tone of voice. Don't be sarcastic.

## 3. Don't argue.

**Rationale:**

Accepting criticism without arguing shows that you are mature.

## Helpful hints:

- Stay calm.
- Try to learn from what the person is saying so you can do a better job next time.
- Remember that the person who is giving you criticism is only trying to help.
- If you disagree, wait until later to discuss the matter.

## BASIC – SKILL 6
# Disagreeing appropriately

---

## 1. Look at the person.

**Rationale:**

Looking at the person shows that you are paying attention.

**Helpful hints:**

- Don't stare or make faces.
- Keep looking at the person throughout your conversation.
- Be pleasant and smile.
- Look at the person as you would a friend.

## 2. Use a pleasant voice.

**Rationale:**

The person is more likely to listen to you if you use a pleasant voice.

**Helpful hints:**

- Speak slowly and clearly. Don't mumble.
- Use short sentences. They are easily understood.
- Keep a comfortable distance between you and the other person while you are talking.
- Smile. People are more comfortable talking with someone who is friendly.

## 3. Say "I understand how you feel."

**Rationale:**

Saying you understand gets the conversation off to a positive start.

**Helpful hints:**

- Plan what you are going to say before you start to speak.
- If you still feel uneasy about how you are going to start your conversation, practice.
- Start to discuss your concerns as part of a conversation, not a confrontation.
- Be sincere.

## 4. Tell why you feel differently.

### Rationale:

Using specific words and reasons avoids confusion and gets your point across.

### Helpful hints:

- Use as much detailed information as possible.
- Be prepared to back up what you say.
- If necessary, practice what you are going to say.
- Always remember to think before you speak.

## 5. Give a reason.

### Rationale:

Your disagreement will carry more weight if you give a valid reason.

### Helpful hints:

- Be sure that your reasons make sense.
- Support your reasons with facts and details.
- One or two reasons are usually enough.
- Remember to stay calm during the conversation.

## 6. Listen to the other person.

### Rationale:

Listening shows you respect what the other person has to say.

### Helpful hints:

- Don't look away or make faces while the other person is talking.
- Don't interrupt.
- Stay calm.
- Don't argue.

## BASIC – SKILL 7
# Showing respect

---

## 1. Obey a request to stop a negative behavior.

### Rationale:

When you obey a request to stop a negative behavior, you show that you can follow instructions. Being able to follow instructions is one form of showing respect.

### Helpful hints:

- By stopping your negative behavior, you may avoid getting into trouble.
- There will always be people who have authority over you. You must do what they say.

## 2. Refrain from teasing, threatening, or making fun of others.

### Rationale:

By refraining from such behaviors, it shows you understand that teasing, threatening, and making fun can be hurtful to others.

### Helpful hints:

- If you are always making fun of people or threatening them, you won't have many friends.
- People will think of you only as a tease, not as a nice person.

## 3. Allow others to have their privacy.

### Rationale:

Sometimes people need or want to be alone. You show respect by following their wishes.

### Helpful hints:

- Always knock before entering someone's room or a room with a closed door.
- Honor someone's desire to be left alone.

## 4. Obtain permission before using another person's property.

### Rationale:

You have certain possessions that are very important to you. You don't want people using them without permission. When you ask permission to use others' things, you show that same kind of respect.

### Helpful hints:

- Always return items in the same condition as when you borrowed them.
- If you damage a borrowed item, offer to repair or replace it.

## 5. Do not damage or vandalize public property.

### Rationale:

Vandalism and damaging property are against the law. Besides getting into trouble, you show disrespect for your community and country when you vandalize public property.

### Helpful hints:

- Accidents do happen, but they always should be reported.
- Offer to replace or repair property you have damaged.

## 6. Refrain from conning or persuading others into breaking rules.

### Rationale:

People will think less of you if you are always trying to take advantage of others or get them into trouble.

### Helpful hints:

- If you use people, they won't trust you.
- People don't appreciate being manipulated.

# 7. Avoid acting obnoxiously in public.

### Rationale:

You make a good impression with people when you show that you know how to behave and use proper social skills in public.

### Helpful hints:

- Be on your best behavior in public. Don't do things like cursing, swearing, spitting, or belching.
- Be courteous to others and mind your manners.

# 8. Dress appropriately when in public.

### Rationale:

When in public, people are expected to look their best. When you live up to this expectation, you show that you are mature and understand society's rules.

### Helpful hints:

- Being well-groomed and well-dressed makes a good impression.
- Use good judgment when deciding what to wear. Where you are going usually determines what you wear.

## BASIC – SKILL 8
# Showing sensitivity to others

---

**1.** **Express interest and concern for others, especially when they are having troubles.**

### Rationale:
If you help others, they are more likely to help you.

### Helpful hints:
- If you see someone in trouble, ask if you can help.
- Sometimes, just showing you care is enough to help a person get through a difficult time.

**2.** **Recognize that disabled people deserve the same respect as anyone else.**

### Rationale:
A disability does not make a person inferior. Helping people with disabilities without ridiculing or patronizing them shows that you believe all people are equal, although some people need a little extra assistance.

### Helpful hints:
- Be ready to help a disabled person when needed by doing such things as holding open a door, carrying a package, or giving up your seat.
- Don't stare at disabled people or make comments about their special needs.

**3.** **Apologize or make amends for hurting someone's feelings or causing harm.**

### Rationale:
Saying you're sorry shows that you can take responsibility for your actions and can admit when you've done something wrong.

### Helpful hints:

- You can harm someone by what you fail to do, just as easily as by what you do. Some examples are breaking a promise or not sticking up for someone who is being picked on.

- If you hurt someone, apologize immediately and sincerely.

## 4. Recognize that people of different races, religions, and backgrounds deserve to be treated the same way as you would expect to be treated.

### Rationale:

Treating others equally shows that although people are different, you believe that it shouldn't matter in the way you treat them.

### Helpful hints:

- Don't make jokes and rude comments about the color of someone's skin or what he or she believes.

- Some people have different customs for doing things. Some people have more money than others. No matter, all people should be treated the same.

# Accepting apologies from others

1. Look at the person who is apologizing.

2. Listen to what he or she is saying.

3. Remain calm. Refrain from making sarcastic statements.

4. Thank the person for the apology; say "Thanks for saying 'I'm sorry'" or "That's okay."

# Accepting compliments

**1.** Look at the person who is complimenting you.

**2.** Use a pleasant tone of voice.

**3.** Thank the person sincerely for the compliment.

**4.** Say "Thanks for noticing" or "I appreciate that."

**5.** Avoid looking away, mumbling, or denying the compliment.

# Accepting consequences

**1.** Look at the person.

**2.** Say "Okay."

**3.** Don't argue.

**4.** If given instructions or suggestions on how to correct the situation, follow them.

# Accepting decisions of authority

**1.** Look at the person.

**2.** Remain calm and monitor your feelings and behavior.

**3.** Use a pleasant or neutral tone of voice.

**4.** Acknowledge the decision by saying "Okay" or "Yes, I understand."

**5.** If you disagree, do so at a later time.

**6.** Refrain from arguing, pouting, or becoming angry.

# Answering the telephone

**1.** Pick up the phone promptly.

**2.** Use a calm, pleasant voice.

**3.** Answer the phone by saying "Hello" or "Hello, this is the residence of…."

**4.** Listen carefully to the other person.

**5.** Find the person the caller wants to speak with or offer to take a message.

**6.** Write the message down and ensure that the right person receives it.

**7.** End your conversation by saying "Good-bye" or "Thanks for calling," and gently hanging up the phone.

# Asking for clarification

**1.** Look at the person.

**2.** Ask if he or she has time to talk. Don't interrupt.

**3.** Use a pleasant or neutral tone of voice.

**4.** Specifically state what you are confused about. Begin with "I was wondering if..." or "Could I ask about...?"

**5.** Listen to the other person's reply and acknowledge the answer.

**6.** Thank the person for his or her time.

# Asking for help

1. Look at the person.

2. Ask the person if he or she has time to help you (now or later).

3. Clearly describe the problem or what kind of help you need.

4. Thank the person for helping you.

# Asking questions

1. **Appropriately get the other person's attention without interrupting. Wait to be acknowledged.**

2. **Look at the person.**

3. **Use a pleasant tone of voice.**

4. **Phrase what you are asking as a question by using words such as "Please," "Would," "What," or "May I...."**

5. **Listen to the person's answer.**

6. **Thank the person for his or her time.**

# Being on time (Promptness)

**1.** Know exactly when you need to be where you are going, and how long it will take you to get there.

**2.** Leave with plenty of time to spare (usually about 5-10 minutes before you would have to leave).

**3.** Go directly to your destination with no diversions.

**4.** When you arrive, check in with someone in authority or with the person you are meeting.

**5.** If you are late, apologize sincerely for not being on time.

# Checking in (or Checking back)

1. Promptly return or complete the task.

2. Immediately find the appropriate person to check with.

3. Check in by pleasantly saying "Here I am..." or "I'm back from...."

4. Truthfully answer any questions about your activities or where you have been.

5. End by saying "Is there anything else?"

# Choosing appropriate words to say

**1.** Look at the situation and the people around you.

**2.** Know the meanings of words you are about to say.

**3.** Refrain from using words that will offend people around you or that they will not understand.

**4.** Avoid using slang, profanity, or words that could have a sexual meaning.

**5.** Decide what thought you want to put into words and then say the words.

# Closing a conversation

**1.** Change topics only when everyone appears to be done talking about a particular issue.

**2.** Change to a conversation topic that somehow relates to the previous one, if possible.

**3.** Allow everyone present a chance to talk about the current topic.

**4.** If it is time to depart or move to another area, wait for a comfortable break in the conversation.

**5.** Stand and say "Excuse me..." or "It was very nice talking to you...."

# Completing homework

---

**1.** Find out at school what the day's homework is for each subject.

**2.** Remember to bring home necessary books or materials in order to complete your assignments.

**3.** Get started on homework promptly, or at the designated time.

**4.** Complete all assignments accurately and neatly.

**5.** Carefully store completed homework until the next school day.

# Completing tasks

**1.** Listen carefully to instructions or directions for tasks.

**2.** Assemble the necessary tools or materials needed for the task.

**3.** Begin working carefully and neatly.

**4.** Remain focused on the task until it is completed.

**5.** Examine the product of your work to make sure it is complete.

**6.** Check back with the person who assigned the task.

# Complying with reasonable requests

**1.** Look at the person making the request.

**2.** Use a pleasant or neutral tone of voice.

**3.** Acknowledge the request by saying "Okay" or "Sure."

**4.** Promptly complete the requested activity.

**5.** If you are unable to do so, politely tell the person that you cannot do what he or she requested.

# Contributing to discussions (Joining in a conversation)

**1.** Look at the people who are talking.

**2.** Wait for a point when no one else is talking.

**3.** Make a short, appropriate comment that relates to the topic being discussed.

**4.** Choose words that will not be offensive or confusing to others.

**5.** Give other people a chance to participate.

# Correcting another person (or Giving criticism)

**1.** Look at the person.

**2.** Remain calm and use a pleasant voice tone.

**3.** Begin with a positive statement, some praise, or by saying "I understand...."

**4.** Be specific about the behaviors you are criticizing.

**5.** Offer a rationale for why this is a problem.

**6.** Listen to the other person's explanation. Avoid any sarcasm, name-calling, or "put-down" statements.

# Doing good quality work

**1.** Find out the exact expectations or instructions for tasks.

**2.** Assemble the necessary tools or materials.

**3.** Carefully begin working. Focus your attention on the task.

**4.** Continue working until the task is completed or criteria are met.

**5.** Examine the results of your work to make sure it was done correctly.

**6.** Correct any deficiencies, if necessary. Perhaps, check back with the person who assigned the task.

# Following rules

---

**1.** Learn what rules apply to the current situation.

**2.** Adjust your behavior so that you are following those rules exactly.

**3.** Don't "bend" rules, even just a little.

**4.** If you have questions, find the appropriate adult to ask about the rules in question.

# Following written instructions

**1.** Read the written instructions for the task one time completely.

**2.** Do what each instruction tells you to in the exact order in which it is written.

**3.** Don't change written instructions or skip any without permission.

**4.** If you have any questions, find the appropriate adult to ask about the instructions in question.

# Getting another person's attention

**1.** Wait until the other person is finished speaking or is available to you.

**2.** Look at the other person.

**3.** Get that person's attention by saying "Excuse me...."

**4.** Wait until he or she acknowledges you. Say what you want to say.

# Getting the teacher's attention

**1.** Look at the teacher.

**2.** Raise your hand calmly.

**3.** Wait to be acknowledged by the teacher.

**4.** Ask questions or make requests in a calm voice.

# Giving compliments

**1.** Look at the person you are complimenting.

**2.** Speak with a clear, enthusiastic voice.

**3.** Praise the person's activity or project specifically. Tell him or her exactly what you like about it.

**4.** Use words such as "That's great," "Wonderful," or "That was awesome."

**5.** Give the other person time to respond to your compliment.

# Greeting others

**1.** Look at the person.

**2.** Use a pleasant voice.

**3.** Say "Hi" or "Hello."

# Ignoring distractions by others

**1.** Try not to look at people who are being distracting.

**2.** Stay focused on your work or task.

**3.** Do not respond to questions, teasing, or giggling.

**4.** If necessary, report this behavior to a nearby adult or authority figure.

# Initiating a conversation

**1.** Look at the person or people you are talking with.

**2.** Wait until no one else is talking about another topic.

**3.** Use a calm, pleasant voice tone.

**4.** Ask a question of the other person or begin talking about a new conversation topic.

**5.** Make sure new conversation topics are about appropriate activities and will not offend other people.

# Interrupting appropriately

**1.** If you must interrupt a person's conversation or phone call, stand where you can be seen.

**2.** Wait for that person to acknowledge you or signal for you to come back later.

**3.** When it's time for you to speak, begin with "Excuse me for interrupting, but...."

**4.** Be specific and to the point with your request or information.

**5.** Thank the person for his or her time.

# Introducing others

**1.** Position yourself near or between the people you are introducing.

**2.** Use a clear, enthusiastic voice tone.

**3.** Introduce two people by saying each person's first and last names. For example, say "Bill, I'd like you to meet Jeff Thompson. Jeff, this is Bill Smith."

**4.** Allow time for each person to shake hands, greet each other, etc.

**5.** You also may provide more information about each person to the other (their jobs, schools, where they are from, etc.).

# Listening to others

**1.** Look at the person who is talking.

**2.** Sit or stand quietly; avoid fidgeting, yawning, or giggling.

**3.** Wait until the person is finished speaking before you speak.

**4.** Show that you understand (say "Okay," "Thanks," or "I see").

# Maintaining a conversation

**1.** Continue looking at whomever is speaking.

**2.** Maintain a relaxed, but attentive, posture. Nod your head to show ongoing acknowledgment.

**3.** Ask follow-up questions that pertain to what the other person just said and show attentiveness.

**4.** Avoid fidgeting, looking away, or yawning.

**5.** Don't interrupt the other person. If interruptions occur, say "Excuse me" and let the other person speak.

**6.** Tell your own stories that pertain to the current topic, but be careful not to dominate the conversation or exaggerate.

# Maintaining an appropriate appearance

**1.** Use appropriate daily hygiene skills.

**2.** Comb your hair.

**3.** Choose clean clothing that will match your day's activities.

**4.** Use a moderate amount of make-up, perfume, or cologne.

**5.** Ask for advice if you are unsure what is proper.

**6.** Maintain your appearance throughout the day (hair combed, shirt tucked in, etc.).

# Maintaining personal hygiene

**1.** Bathe or shower daily.

**2.** Brush your teeth in the morning and at bedtime.

**3.** Brush or comb your hair.

**4.** Put on clean clothes daily.

**5.** Wash your hands before meals and after using the bathroom.

**6.** Put dirty clothes in the hamper.

# Making an apology

**1.** Look at the person.

**2.** Use a serious, sincere voice tone, but don't pout.

**3.** Begin by saying "I wanted to apologize for..." or "I'm sorry for...."

**4.** Do not make excuses or try to rationalize your behavior.

**5.** Sincerely say that you will try not to repeat the same behavior in the future.

**6.** Offer to compensate or pay restitution.

**7.** Thank the other person for listening.

# Making a request (Asking a favor)

**1.** Look at the person.

**2.** Use a clear, pleasant voice tone.

**3.** Make your request in the form of a question by saying "Would you..." and "Please...."

**4.** If your request is granted, remember to say "Thank you."

**5.** If your request is denied, remember to accept "No" for an answer.

# Making a telephone call

---

**1.** Accurately identify the number you need to call.

**2.** Dial the number carefully.

**3.** Ask to speak to the person you are calling by saying "May I please speak to...?"

**4.** Use appropriate language over the phone; no obscenities or sexually oriented words.

**5.** If the person you are calling is not there, ask the person who answers if he or she will take a message.

**6.** At the end of your conversation, thank the person for his or her time.

# Making positive self-statements

**1.** Make positive statements about actual accomplishments.

**2.** Don't lie or exaggerate.

**3.** Begin by saying in a pleasant tone of voice "I'm proud of..." or "I think I did well at...."

**4.** Don't brag about yourself or put down other people's efforts.

# Making positive statements about others

**1.** Try to notice or find out positive things or events about others.

**2.** Use a clear, enthusiastic tone of voice.

**3.** Praise a specific trait or ability of the other person, or congratulate him or her on a recent accomplishment.

**4.** Don't say anything that would invalidate your compliment, such as "It's about time...."

# Offering assistance or help

**1.** Ask the other person if he or she needs help.

**2.** Listen to what the person needs.

**3.** Offer to help in ways that you can.

**4.** Do what you agree to do for that person.

# Participating in activities

**1.** Appropriately request to be a part of an activity.

**2.** Cooperate with others in the group, such as allowing others to take their turns.

**3.** Use a pleasant voice when talking to others.

**4.** Remember to accept losing or winning appropriately.

# Refraining from possessing contraband or drugs

**1.** Refuse to accept drugs or contraband from strangers, acquaintances, or peers.

**2.** Examine your own possessions and decide whether they are appropriate to have (legally, morally, rightfully yours).

**3.** Turn in drugs or contraband to the appropriate adult or authority figure.

**4.** Self-report your involvement; peer report, if necessary.

**5.** Honestly answer any questions that are asked.

# Reporting emergencies

**1.** Identify exactly what the emergency is.

**2.** Immediately find a responsible adult or police officer, or call 911.

**3.** Specifically state who and where you are.

**4.** Specifically describe the emergency situation.

# Reporting other youths' behavior (or Peer reporting)

**1.** Find the appropriate adult or authority figure.

**2.** Look at the person.

**3.** Use a clear, concerned voice tone.

**4.** State specifically the inappropriate behavior you are reporting.

**5.** Give a reason for the report that shows concern for your peer.

**6.** Truthfully answer any questions that are asked of you.

# Resisting peer pressure

**1.** Look at the person.

**2.** Use a calm, assertive voice tone.

**3.** State clearly that you do not want to engage in the inappropriate activity.

**4.** Suggest an alternative activity. Give a reason.

**5.** If the person persists, continue to say "No."

**6.** If the peer will not accept your "No" answer, ask him or her to leave or remove yourself from the situation.

# Saying good-bye to guests

**1.** Stand up and accompany guests to the door.

**2.** Look at the person.

**3.** Use a pleasant voice tone.

**4.** Extend your hand and shake hands firmly.

**5.** Say "Good-bye, thank you for visiting" or "Goodbye (name), it was nice to meet you."

**6.** Ask the guests to return in the future.

# Saying "No" assertively

**1.** Look at the person.

**2.** Use a clear, firm voice tone.

**3.** Say "No, I don't want...."

**4.** Request that the person leave you alone.

**5.** Remain calm, but serious.

**6.** If necessary, remove yourself from the situation.

# Seeking positive attention

**1.** Wait until the adult or authority figure has time to attend to you.

**2.** Look at the person.

**3.** Wait for acknowledgment.

**4.** Appropriately ask for time to talk.

**5.** Discuss positive events or activities.

**6.** Do not seek attention by whining, pouting, or begging.

# Showing appreciation

**1.** Look at the person.

**2.** Use a pleasant, sincere voice tone.

**3.** Say "Thank you for..." and specifically describe what the person did that you appreciate.

**4.** If appropriate, give a reason for why it was so beneficial.

**5.** Offer future help or favors on your part.

# Showing interest

**1.** Look at the person who is talking.

**2.** Give quiet acknowledgments, such as nodding your head or saying "Uh huh."

**3.** Acknowledge specifically by saying "That's interesting...."

**4.** Ask follow-up questions for more information.

# Staying on task

**1.** Look at your task or assignment.

**2.** Think about the steps needed to complete the task.

**3.** Focus all of your attention on your task.

**4.** Stop working on your task only with permission from the nearby adult who gave you the task.

**5.** Ignore distractions and interruptions by others.

# Trying new tasks

**1.** Identify a new task or activity you've never done before.

**2.** Request permission from the appropriate person.

**3.** Think of all the steps needed for the new task.

**4.** Breathe deeply and try your best.

**5.** Ask for help, advice, or feedback if the task is difficult.

# Using an appropriate voice tone

**1.** Look at the person you are talking to.

**2.** Listen to the level and quality of the voice tone you are speaking with.

**3.** Lower your voice (if necessary) so that it isn't too loud or harsh.

**4.** Speak slowly. Think about what you want to say.

**5.** Concentrate on making your voice sound calm, neutral, or even pleasant and happy.

**6.** Avoid shouting, whining, or begging.

# Using anger control strategies

**1.** If a person is talking to you, continue listening and acknowledging what he or she is saying.

**2.** Monitor your body's feelings and how quickly you are breathing.

**3.** Breathe slowly and deeply.

**4.** Give yourself instructions to continue breathing deeply and relax your tense body areas.

**5.** If appropriate, calmly ask the other person for a few minutes to be by yourself.

**6.** While you are alone, continue to monitor your feelings and instruct yourself to relax.

# Using structured problem-solving (SODAS)

**1.** Define the problem <u>S</u>ituation.

**2.** Generate two or more <u>O</u>ptions.

**3.** Look at each option's potential <u>D</u>isadvantages.

**4.** Look at each option's potential <u>A</u>dvantages.

**5.** Decide on the best <u>S</u>olution.

# Using table etiquette

**1.** Sit quietly at the table with your hands in your lap.

**2.** Place your napkin in your lap.

**3.** Offer food and beverages to guests first.

**4.** When requesting food, remember to say "Please" and "Thank you."

**5.** Engage in appropriate mealtime conversation topics.

**6.** Avoid belching, taking large bites of food, talking with your mouth full, or grabbing food with your fingers.

**7.** When you've finished eating, ask permission to be excused and offer to clear your guests' plates.

# Volunteering

1. Look at the person.

2. Use a clear, enthusiastic voice tone.

3. Ask to volunteer for a specific activity or task.

4. Thank the person and check back when the task is completed.

# Waiting your turn

---

**1.** Sit or stand quietly.

**2.** Keep your arms and legs still. Do not fidget.

**3.** Avoid sighing, whining, or begging.

**4.** Engage in the activity when directed to do so by an adult.

**5.** Thank the person who gives you a turn.

# Accepting defeat or loss

**1.** Look at the person or members of the team who won.

**2.** Remain calm and positive.

**3.** Say "Good game" or "Congratulations."

**4.** Reward yourself for trying your hardest.

# Accepting help or assistance

**1.** Look at the person offering help.

**2.** Sincerely thank him or her for helping. If help is not needed, politely decline the person's assistance.

**3.** If help is needed, accept the help or advice and again thank the person.

# Accepting winning appropriately

**1.** Look at the person or members of the team who lost.

**2.** Remain pleasant but not overly happy or celebratory.

**3.** Congratulate the other person or team for a good game and for trying.

**4.** Do not brag or boast about winning.

# Advocating for oneself

**1.** Identify a situation in which you should advocate for yourself.

**2.** Remember to remain calm and use a pleasant or neutral voice tone.

**3.** Describe your point of view or the outcome you desire.

**4.** Give rationales for advocating for yourself.

**5.** Thank the person for listening.

# Analyzing skills needed for different situations

**1.** Look at the immediate situation facing you.

**2.** Define the situation by what is occurring (i.e., people are giving you criticism, people are giving instructions, people are introducing themselves, etc.).

**3.** Match a curriculum skill or skills to the situation (i.e., Following Instructions, Accepting Criticism, greeting skills, etc.).

**4.** Perform the steps of the appropriate skill.

# Analyzing social situations

**1.** Think about the people you are getting ready to encounter.

**2.** Look at the situation that is occurring.

**3.** Think about appropriate behaviors you have learned in the past.

**4.** Choose the behaviors that seem the most appropriate for the situation and people you are dealing with.

# Analyzing tasks to be completed

**1.** Clarify what task or assignment has been given to you.

**2.** List every step that you need to do in order to complete the task.

**3.** Identify which step needs to be done first, second, third, etc.

**4.** Begin completing the steps in order.

# Being prepared for class

**1.** Gather all necessary books, papers, homework, and writing implements.

**2.** Be on time for class.

**3.** Present homework and assignments when the teacher asks for them.

**4.** Write down assignments and homework to complete.

ADVANCED – SKILL 73

# Borrowing from others

**1.** Appropriately ask to borrow something from another person.

**2.** Accept "No" if the person declines.

**3.** If the person agrees, find out when you need to return the possession you are borrowing.

**4.** Care for others' property while you have it and promptly return it when you are finished.

# Caring for others' property

**1.** Use others' property only with their permission.

**2.** Make an appropriate request if you want to use something that belongs to another person.

**3.** Use others' property only as it is supposed to be used or according to instructions.

**4.** Take care of others' property as if it was your own.

**5.** If something gets broken, apologize and offer to replace it.

# Caring for own belongings

---

**1.** Use your own property as it is supposed to be used or according to instructions.

**2.** Avoid needlessly tearing, writing on, or breaking your possessions.

**3.** When you're done, return possessions to the appropriate place.

**4.** If something gets broken, tell an adult.

# Choosing appropriate clothing

---

**1.** Think about what situations and activities will occur during the day.

**2.** Choose clothing that suits the season.

**3.** Match colors and styles.

**4.** Do not wear clothing that is too revealing or associated with gang activities, alcohol, drugs, or cigarettes.

**5.** Care for your clothing throughout the day. Do not cut, tear, or write on clothing.

# Choosing appropriate friends

**1.** Think of the qualities and interests you would look for in a friend.

**2.** Look at the strengths and weaknesses of potential friends.

**3.** Match the characteristics of potential friends with activities and interests you would share.

**4.** Avoid peers who are involved with drugs, gangs, or breaking the law.

ADVANCED – SKILL 78

# Communicating honestly

**1.** Look at the person.

**2.** Use a clear voice. Avoid stammering or hesitating.

**3.** Respond to questions factually and completely.

**4.** Do not leave out details or important facts.

**5.** Truthfully take responsibility for any inappropriate behaviors you displayed.

# Complying with school dress code

**1.** Know the clothing limits of your school.

**2.** Choose clothing that matches those limits.

**3.** Do not tear or write on your clothing at school.

**4.** Do not change what you are wearing to school (add or subtract clothing) without telling the adults who are responsible for you.

# Compromising with others

**1.** Identify disagreements before they get out of hand.

**2.** Suggest alternative activities that you and your peer could agree to do.

**3.** Listen to what your peer suggests.

**4.** Remain calm and continue to talk about a compromise.

# Concentrating on a subject or task

**1.** Promptly begin work on a task.

**2.** Focus your attention directly on the subject.

**3.** If your attention wanders, instruct yourself to concentrate on the task.

**4.** Ignore distractions or interruptions by others.

**5.** Remain on task until the work is completed.

# Contributing to group activities

**1.** Appropriately request to join in an activity.

**2.** Ask what role you can play.

**3.** Do your job thoroughly and completely.

**4.** Cooperate with others by listening and accepting feedback.

**5.** Praise others' performance and share credit for the outcome.

# Controlling eating habits

**1.** Eat mainly at mealtimes and limit between-meal snacks.

**2.** Eat slowly, putting your knife and fork down between bites.

**3.** Limit yourself to reasonable portions and few second helpings.

**4.** Do not eat impulsively or when you are anxious or frustrated.

**5.** Ask for help from a caring adult if eating habits get out of control.

# Controlling emotions

**1.** Learn what situations cause you to lose control or make you angry.

**2.** Monitor the feelings you have in stressful situations.

**3.** Instruct yourself to breathe deeply and relax when stressful feelings begin to arise.

**4.** Reword angry feelings so they can be expressed appropriately and calmly to others.

**5.** Praise yourself for controlling emotional outbursts.

# Controlling sexually abusive impulses toward others

**1.** Identify sexual feelings or fantasies about others as they occur.

**2.** Instruct yourself to consider the consequences of acting on these impulses to you and the other person.

**3.** Prompt yourself to not act on sexually abusive feelings. Remember what sexual abuse does to young children.

**4.** Redirect your thoughts to other things or more appropriate behaviors.

**5.** Ask for help from a caring adult to deal with sexually abusive impulses.

# Controlling the impulse to lie

**1.** Identify untrue statements before you say them.

**2.** Stop talking and pause.

**3.** Answer all questions factually and make only truthful statements.

**4.** Consider the long-term consequences of lying to others.

**5.** Apologize for any untrue statements that you previously made.

# Controlling the impulse to steal

**1.** Identify and avoid situations in which you are likely to steal.

**2.** Before you steal, stop your behaviors immediately.

**3.** Instruct yourself to leave the area without stealing.

**4.** Consider the long-term consequences of stealing.

**5.** Self-report any previous stealing.

# Cooperating with others

**1.** Discuss mutual goals or tasks with others.

**2.** Know what you must do to help accomplish those goals.

**3.** Give and accept constructive criticism appropriately with peers.

**4.** Follow rules if you are playing a game and share resources with others.

**5.** Praise peers' efforts and cooperation.

# Coping with anger and aggression from others

**1.** Look at the person.

**2.** Remain calm and take deep breaths.

**3.** Use a neutral voice and facial expression; no laughing or smirking.

**4.** Avoid critical or sarcastic comments.

**5.** Listen to and acknowledge what the other person is saying.

**6.** If the other person becomes aggressive or abusive, leave the situation.

**7.** Report the incident to an adult.

# Coping with change

**1.** Identify exactly what is changing.

**2.** Ask questions for clarification.

**3.** Remain calm and relaxed.

**4.** Appropriately discuss your feelings about the change with a caring adult.

**5.** Avoid becoming unmotivated or depressed.

# Coping with conflict

**1.** Remain calm and relaxed.

**2.** Listen to what the persons in conflict are saying.

**3.** Think of helpful options.

**4.** If appropriate, offer options to the people who are involved in the conflict.

**5.** If the situation becomes aggressive or dangerous, remove yourself.

# Coping with sad feelings (or depression)

**1.** Identify what situations tend to make you sad.

**2.** Acknowledge sad feelings when they arise.

**3.** Report your feelings to a caring adult or peer.

**4.** Find alternative activities that you enjoy and participate in them. Get outside for fresh air and sunshine.

**5.** Avoid isolating yourself or withdrawing from friends and relatives.

**6.** Discuss sad feelings openly and frankly.

# Dealing with an accusation

**1.** Look at the person with a neutral facial expression.

**2.** Remain calm and monitor your feelings and behavior.

**3.** Listen carefully to what the other person is saying.

**4.** Acknowledge what the person is saying or that a problem exists.

**5.** Ask if this is the appropriate time to respond. Say "May I respond to what you are saying?"

**6.** If the person says "Yes," respond truthfully and factually by either self-reporting, peer reporting, or honestly denying the accusation.

**7.** If the person says "No," delay your appropriate disagreement to a later time and continue to listen and acknowledge.

# Dealing with being left out

**1.** Accurately identify that you have been left out or excluded.

**2.** Remain calm and monitor your own feelings and behavior.

**3.** Either find another positive activity to engage in or locate an adult to talk with.

**4.** Possibly discuss your feelings with those who initially left you out. Remember to give and accept criticism appropriately.

# Dealing with boredom

---

**1.** Identify the feeling of being bored.

**2.** Look for alternative, appropriate activities.

**3.** If necessary, request permission to participate in other activities.

**4.** Avoid delinquent or gang-related behavior.

# Dealing with contradictory messages

**1.** Identify which messages or people appear to contradict themselves.

**2.** Ask each person for clarification.

**3.** Specifically explain what messages appear contradictory.

**4.** Remember to continue following instructions and delay disagreements.

# Dealing with embarrassing situations

1. Think ahead to avoid as many embarrassments as possible.

2. When embarrassed, remain calm and monitor your feelings and behavior.

3. Continue to breathe deeply and relax.

4. If possible, laugh at yourself and forget about the embarrassing situation.

5. Otherwise, remove yourself from the situation in order to collect your thoughts and to relax.

# Dealing with failure

**1.** Accurately identify that you did not succeed in a particular activity.

**2.** Remain calm and relaxed.

**3.** Instruct yourself to control emotional behavior.

**4.** Find a caring adult and discuss your disappointment or other negative feelings.

**5.** Be willing to try again to be successful.

# Dealing with fear

**1.** Identify what is making you afraid.

**2.** Decide whether you are in danger or just feeling afraid or intimidated.

**3.** Remain calm and relaxed. Continue to breathe deeply.

**4.** Discuss with a caring adult what is causing your fear.

**5.** Instruct yourself to eventually conquer your fears.

# Dealing with frustration

**1.** Identify feelings of frustration as they arise.

**2.** Determine the source of these feelings.

**3.** Breathe deeply and relax when frustrations arise.

**4.** Discuss frustrations with a caring adult or peer.

**5.** Find alternative activities that promote feelings of success.

# Dealing with group pressure

---

**1.** Look at the group.

**2.** Remain calm, but serious.

**3.** Assertively say "No " to inappropriate group activities.

**4.** If possible, suggest an alternative activity.

**5.** Remove yourself if pressure continues.

# Dealing with rejection

**1.** Examine behaviors that may have led to being rejected.

**2.** Remain calm and relaxed.

**3.** Use a neutral tone of voice with the other person.

**4.** Possibly disagree appropriately or give appropriate criticism.

**5.** If rejection continues, remove yourself and engage in alternative activities.

# Delaying gratification

**1.** Identify what you want or what you want to do.

**2.** Instruct yourself to stop behaviors that are inappropriate for the situation.

**3.** Remain calm and relaxed.

**4.** Find alternative activities to substitute.

ADVANCED – SKILL 104
# Displaying effort

**1.** Remain on task and work diligently.

**2.** Do your best to accomplish tasks to criteria.

**3.** Inform others of your efforts, if appropriate.

# Displaying sportsmanship

**1.** Play fair and according to the rules.

**2.** Avoid fighting or criticizing others.

**3.** Remember to accept winning appropriately without bragging.

**4.** Remember to accept losing appropriately without pouting or complaining.

**5.** Thank the other players for participating.

# Expressing appropriate affection

**1.** Identify your relationship with the other person.

**2.** Determine the appropriate boundary or level of closeness between you and the other person.

**3.** Choose the appropriate behaviors to match that level of closeness and the situation.

**4.** Assess the other person's comfort with the situation and your affectionate behaviors.

**5.** Refrain from using overly physical displays of affection in public or with people you have only recently met.

# Expressing feelings appropriately

**1.** Remain calm and relaxed.

**2.** Look at the person you are talking to.

**3.** Describe the feelings you are currently having.

**4.** Avoid profanity and statements of blame.

**5.** Take responsibility for feelings you are having.

**6.** Thank the person for listening.

# Expressing optimism

**1.** Look at the person.

**2.** Use an enthusiastic voice tone.

**3.** Describe potential positive outcomes.

**4.** Express hope and desire for positive outcomes.

**5.** Thank the person for listening.

# Expressing pride in accomplishments

**1.** Look at the person you are talking to.

**2.** Use an enthusiastic voice tone.

**3.** Describe accomplishments and your pride in them.

**4.** Be careful not to brag, boast, or put down others.

# Following safety rules

**1.** Learn the rules that apply to different situations.

**2.** Adjust behaviors according to directives in rules.

**3.** Do not "bend" or test safety rules.

**4.** Report others who break safety rules, for their own good.

# Following through on agreements and contracts

**1.** Avoid making commitments you cannot keep.

**2.** Know exactly what is involved in any agreements you make.

**3.** Do exactly what you committed to do, promptly and completely.

**4.** If you cannot follow through, apologize and offer to compensate.

# Giving instructions

**1.** Look at the person you are instructing.

**2.** Begin with "Please...."

**3.** State specifically what you would like him or her to do.

**4.** Offer rationales, if needed.

**5.** Thank the person for listening and for following your instructions.

# Giving rationales

**1.** Look at the person.

**2.** Explain your point of view with rationales that the other person can understand.

**3.** Use rationales that point out the potential benefit to the other person.

**4.** Ask if the person understands your reasoning.

# Interacting appropriately with members of the opposite sex

**1.** Determine the appropriate level of closeness or boundary that fits the relationship, observing proper moral standards.

**2.** A boundary is an imaginary line that determines the amount of openness and sharing in a relationship.

**3.** In general, boundaries are intellectual, emotional, physical, and spiritual.

**4.** Avoid overly physical displays of affection.

**5.** Avoid jokes or language that are sexually oriented and that may make the other person uncomfortable.

**6.** Do not engage in inappropriate sexual behavior, which includes sexual intercourse, homosexual activity, incest, sexual activity with someone much older or younger, rape, violent or intimidating boy-girl relationships, sexually taking advantage of another person, and overt public displays of affection, such as fondling and petting.

# Keeping property in its place

---

**1.** Know where property is usually kept or belongs.

**2.** Ask the appropriate person for permission to remove property.

**3.** Take care of property you are responsible for.

**4.** Return the property to its place in its original condition.

# Lending to others

---

**1.** If possible, respond to requests of others by saying "Yes."

**2.** Lend only your property or things for which you are responsible.

**3.** Specify when you would like your property returned.

**4.** Thank the other person for returning your property.

# Making decisions

**1.** Accurately identify what decision you must make.

**2.** Examine what your choices currently appear to be.

**3.** Generate other choices, if possible.

**4.** Look at the potential consequences (positive and negative) of each choice.

**5.** Pick the first- and second-best choices based on the potential outcomes.

# Making new friends

**1.** Look at the potential new friend.

**2.** Use a pleasant voice and introduce yourself.

**3.** Share some of your interests and hobbies.

**4.** Listen to the other person's name and areas of interest.

**5.** Plan appropriate activities with permission.

# Making restitution (Compensating)

**1.** Begin by making an appropriate apology.

**2.** Offer to compensate for any offenses you may have committed.

**3.** Follow through on restitution promises.

**4.** Thank the person for allowing you to make compensation.

# Managing time

**1.** List all tasks for a particular day or week.

**2.** Estimate the time needed to complete each task.

**3.** Plan for delays, setbacks, and problems.

**4.** Implement a daily schedule that includes planned tasks.

**5.** Evaluate your time-management plan for effectiveness.

# Negotiating with others

**1.** Calmly explain your viewpoint to the other person.

**2.** Listen to the other person's ideas.

**3.** Offer an alternative or compromise that is mutually beneficial.

**4.** Give rationales for opinions.

**5.** Together choose the best alternative.

**6.** Thank the person for listening.

# Organizing tasks and activities

**1.** List all tasks you are required to do.

**2.** Prioritize tasks based on importance and your abilities and time.

**3.** Complete tasks in the order of priority.

**4.** Manage your time well and avoid putting off tasks until the last minute.

# Persevering on
# tasks and projects

**1.** Know exactly what must be done in order to complete a task or project.

**2.** Get started promptly without procrastinating.

**3.** Remain on task until finished.

**4.** Deal appropriately with frustrations or disappointments.

# Planning meals

---

**1.** Know what food is available or make a grocery list.

**2.** Plan meals based on the four food groups.

**3.** If necessary, ask for suggestions or feedback from roommates.

**4.** Monitor the contents of foods you buy. Avoid foods that are high in fats and carbohydrates.

# Preparing for a stressful conversation

**1.** Remember and practice relaxation strategies.

**2.** Instruct yourself to continue breathing deeply.

**3.** Remember to keep looking at the person and express your feelings appropriately.

**4.** Review skills such as Accepting Criticism, Disagreeing Appropriately, and Solving Problems.

# Preventing trouble with others

**1.** Identify situations that commonly result in conflicts.

**2.** Review the skills that are necessary to handle those specific situations.

**3.** Approach situations with a positive voice, a smile, and a willingness to compromise.

**4.** Ask for advice from a caring adult.

# Problem-solving a disagreement

**1.** Look at the person.

**2.** Remain calm. Use a pleasant voice.

**3.** Identify options for solving the disagreement.

**4.** Consider the potential consequences.

**5.** Choose the best solution for the situation.

**6.** Be open to the other person's views.

# Responding to complaints

**1.** Look at the person.

**2.** Remain calm.

**3.** Listen closely to the person's complaint.

**4.** Express empathy and acknowledge the problem.

**5.** If appropriate, apologize and attempt to correct the problem.

**6.** Delay disagreements until later.

# Responding to others' feelings

**1.** Listen closely to the other person.

**2.** Acknowledge what he or she is saying and feeling.

**3.** Express concern and empathy.

**4.** Offer to help or provide advice, if the other person wants it.

**5.** Encourage the person to seek additional help, if necessary.

# Responding to others' humor

**1.** If the humor is appropriate, laugh accordingly.

**2.** If the humor is inappropriate, ignore it or prompt the person not to make such jokes.

**3.** If inappropriate humor continues, report the other person's behavior to an adult.

# Responding to teasing

**1.** Remain calm, but serious.

**2.** Assertively ask the person to stop teasing.

**3.** If the teasing doesn't stop, ignore the other person or remove yourself.

**4.** If the teasing stops, thank the other person for stopping and explain how teasing makes you feel.

**5.** Report continued teasing or hazing to an adult.

# Responding to written requests

**1.** Read the request completely.

**2.** Ask for clarification, if needed.

**3.** Perform the requests promptly and thoroughly.

**4.** Check back when the task is completed.

# Self-correcting own behavior

**1.** Monitor your behaviors during difficult or stressful circumstances.

**2.** Notice the effects your behaviors have on other people. Notice their response to what you say.

**3.** Instruct yourself to correct behaviors that appear to make others uncomfortable.

**4.** Use new behaviors and note their effects.

**5.** Continue to make adjustments, as necessary.

**6.** Reward yourself for correcting your own behaviors.

# Self-reporting own behaviors

**1.** Find the appropriate person to report to.

**2.** Look at the person.

**3.** Remain calm and use a neutral voice tone.

**4.** Truthfully and completely describe the behaviors you are reporting.

**5.** Honestly answer questions that are asked.

**6.** Peer report, if necessary.

**7.** Avoid making excuses or rationalizing behaviors.

# Setting appropriate boundaries

**1.** Imagine a series of circles radiating out from you. Each represents a boundary.

**2.** Picture people you encounter in one of the circles, depending on the level of closeness with which you and another person are comfortable.

**3.** Disclose personal information only to those in the closest boundaries.

**4.** Touch others only in ways that are appropriate to your boundaries. Also, respect the boundaries of others.

# Sharing attention with others

**1.** Sit or stand quietly while sharing attention.

**2.** Avoid distracting behaviors such as whining, laughing loudly, or complaining.

**3.** Wait until others pause before speaking or participating.

**4.** Contribute to the discussion or activity appropriately.

# Sharing personal experiences

---

**1.** Decide if you should share personal experiences with the other person.

**2.** Determine whether that person appears comfortable with what you are telling him or her.

**3.** Share experiences that are appropriate for another person to know.

**4.** If what you told the other person is confidential, make sure he or she knows that.

# Suggesting an activity

1. **Get the other person's attention.**

2. **Suggest a specific activity or project to engage in.**

3. **Give rationales for your ideas.**

4. **Listen to the other person's opinions.**

# Using appropriate humor

**1.** Use humor only under appropriate circumstances.

**2.** Avoid humor that makes fun of groups in society, handicapped people, or individuals in your peer group.

**3.** Avoid sexually oriented jokes and profanity.

**4.** If humor offends others, promptly and sincerely apologize.

# Using appropriate language

**1.** Choose words that accurately reflect your thoughts and feelings.

**2.** Avoid making blaming statements.

**3.** Know the meaning of words and phrases you choose.

**4.** Avoid profanity, slang, or terms that others may find offensive.

**5.** Frequently ask if you are being clear and understood.

# Using relaxation strategies

**1.** Breathe deeply and completely.

**2.** Tighten and relax any tense body areas.

**3.** Instruct yourself to remain calm.

**4.** Visualize a relaxing scene (e.g., mountains, walking along a beach, etc.).

**5.** At the first sign of increasing stress, say to yourself "3, 2, 1, relax" and continue breathing deeply.

# Using self-talk or self-instruction

**1.** Look at what is happening around you.

**2.** Stop ongoing behaviors that are causing problems.

**3.** Think of the best alternative behavior to engage in.

**4.** Instruct yourself to engage in the appropriate alternative behavior.

**5.** Reward yourself for using self-talk or self-instruction.

# Using spontaneous problem-solving

**1.** Stop ongoing problem behaviors and relax.

**2.** Define the immediate problem situation you face.

**3.** Think of alternative actions and strategies.

**4.** Think of the possible consequences for each option.

**5.** Choose the best strategy for avoiding trouble and improving the situation.

**6.** Use the best strategy and assess the outcome.

**7.** Reward yourself for solving a problem.

# Using study skills

**1.** Gather the necessary books and materials.

**2.** Focus your attention on the required academic work.

**3.** Make notes of important facts.

**4.** Repeat important points to yourself several times.

**5.** Remain on task, free from distractions (no radio or TV on).

# Working independently

**1.** Start on tasks promptly without procrastinating.

**2.** Remain on task without being reminded.

**3.** Continue working unprompted until the task is completed.

**4.** Check back with the person who assigned the task.

# Accepting self

**1.** Accurately identify your own strengths and weaknesses.

**2.** Express appropriate pride in your accomplishments.

**3.** Compensate for weaknesses by accentuating your strengths.

**4.** Use self-accepting phrases when talking about your tastes, style, etc.

# Altering one's environment

**1.** Identify situations in which you encounter difficulty.

**2.** Look for parts of those situations that could be changed to bring about improvement.

**3.** Make appropriate changes to improve self-esteem, behavior, and performance.

# Asking for advice

---

**1.** Identify a person who is qualified to give you advice.

**2.** Ask the person if he or she has time to talk.

**3.** Specifically describe the situation in which you need help.

**4.** Listen closely to the advice.

**5.** Thank the person for his or her time.

**6.** If the advice appears useful, implement the suggestions.

# Assessing own abilities

**1.** Make a list of your strengths and weaknesses.

**2.** List situations in which you have been successful or have had problems.

**3.** Plan future activities in consideration of your abilities.

## COMPLEX – SKILL 150

# Being an appropriate role model

---

**1.** Identify a situation that requires you to appropriately model behavior for younger peers or siblings.

**2.** Engage in positive interactions with adults or peers. Initiate only appropriate conversation topics.

**3.** Refrain from inappropriate language, sexual behavior, delinquency, bullying, etc.

**4.** Correct peer behavior in a positive, constructive manner.

**5.** Remember that inappropriate role-modeling can negatively affect younger children.

# Being a consumer

1. Know the contents of food and beverages you buy.

2. Look for ways to save money through sales, buying store brands, using coupons, etc.

3. If a store sells you a defective product, return it and appropriately request a refund.

4. Keep track of receipts, warranties, etc.

5. Learn what rights consumers have.

# Being assertive

---

**1.** Look at the person.

**2.** Use a neutral, calm voice.

**3.** Remain relaxed and breathe deeply.

**4.** Clearly state your opinion or disagreement.
Avoid emotional terms.

**5.** Listen to the other person.

**6.** Acknowledge his or her viewpoints and opinions.

**7.** Thank the person for listening.

## COMPLEX – SKILL 153

# Being patient

---

**1.** Sit or stand quietly.

**2.** Wait until your turn or until you are called on.

**3.** Avoid making loud complaints or becoming angry.

**4.** Disagree appropriately later on.

# Budgeting and managing money

**1.** Assess your consistent weekly or monthly income.

**2.** List all of the bills or expenses you have to pay during that time period.

**3.** Estimate the costs of appropriate leisure time activities and entertainment.

**4.** Set aside 10% of your income for unexpected needs or to put into a savings account.

**5.** Stay within the budget you have developed.

**6.** Refrain from impulsively spending money or writing checks.

# Clarifying values and beliefs

**1.** Decide what behaviors you consider to be appropriate or inappropriate.

**2.** Learn how your behavior affects other people.

**3.** Decide what characteristics about yourself you value and don't want to change.

**4.** Decide if you have characteristics that you do not value and would like to change.

**5.** Picture the type of person you want to be and how this would affect others.

# Differentiating friends from acquaintances

**1.** For each person you know, think about how long you have known him or her.

**2.** Identify the activities you may engage in with each friend or acquaintance.

**3.** Share personal information only with people you know as close friends.

**4.** Avoid compromising situations (e.g., accepting rides, dating, drinking) with people you have known for only a short time.

# Displaying appropriate control

**1.** Monitor your feelings and your verbal and nonverbal behavior.

**2.** Use relaxation strategies to manage stress.

**3.** Speak calmly, clearly, and specifically.

**4.** Accurately represent your feelings with well-chosen words.

**5.** Use language that will not offend others.

# Expressing empathy and understanding for others

**1.** Listen closely as the other person expresses his or her feelings.

**2.** Express empathy by saying, "I understand...."

**3.** Demonstrate concern through your words and actions.

**4.** Reflect back the other person's words by saying, "It seems like you're saying...."

**5.** Offer any help or assistance you can.

# Expressing grief

---

**1.** Find an appropriate person to talk to.

**2.** Discuss your feelings of grief.

**3.** Feel free to cry or release hurt feelings as needed.

**4.** Ask for advice, if needed.

**5.** If needed, seek professional assistance.

# Formulating strategies

**1.** Decide on the goal or product.

**2.** Analyze the critical steps in accomplishing the goal.

**3.** List any alternative strategies.

**4.** Implement the best plan and follow through to completion.

# Gathering information

**1.** Know your topic or what you need information about.

**2.** Go to the school or local library, or use appropriate online search engines.

**3.** Ask for help from library reference staff, if needed.

**4.** Assemble materials.

**5.** Write down or copy the information you need.

# Identifying own feelings

**1.** Examine how you are currently feeling.

**2.** List how your feelings change with different situations and experiences.

**3.** Monitor your physical feelings and your emotions when you actually encounter these situations.

**4.** Correctly identify and label various feelings as they arise.

**5.** Communicate your feelings so they can be understood by others.

# Interviewing for a job

**1.** Dress neatly and appropriately for the interview.

**2.** Introduce yourself enthusiastically to the interviewer.

**3.** Answer all questions honestly and calmly.

**4.** Emphasize your strengths, as well as what you would still need to learn.

**5.** Ask any questions you have about the job at the conclusion of the interview.

**6.** Thank the person for his or her time.

# Laughing at oneself

**1.** Identify a situation that previously may have caused you embarrassment or discomfort.

**2.** Look for the humor in these situations.

**3.** Be willing to laugh at your mistakes or imperfections.

# Maintaining relationships

1. **Frequently ask for feedback from others and be willing to accept it.**

2. **Express concern and appropriate affection.**

3. **Negotiate and compromise on activities.**

4. **Share attention with others and avoid possessive or exclusionary behaviors.**

# Making an appropriate complaint

**1.** Look at the person.

**2.** Phrase your complaint as an objective problem, not a personal attack.

**3.** Remain calm and pleasant.

**4.** Be assertive, but avoid repeating your complaint over and over.

**5.** Thank the person for his or her cooperation.

# Making moral and spiritual decisions

**1.** Identify your values regarding life, sexuality, and intimacy.

**2.** Remember that your values should be expressed in your behavior.

**3.** Do not use people for your own personal or sexual gratification.

**4.** Behave in ways that demonstrate your respect for fellow human beings and concern for their needs.

# Managing stress

---

**1.** Identify situations and/or circumstances that produce stress.

**2.** Learn your body's responses to stressful situations.

**3.** Use relaxation cues to overcome stress responses.

**4.** Generalize these relaxation cues to the situations that tend to cause stress.

**5.** Reward yourself for using stress-management techniques.

# Planning ahead

**1.** Know your eventual goal or outcome.

**2.** Identify the sequence in which tasks or objectives need to occur.

**3.** Make plans for completing tasks that account for demands on your time.

**4.** Keep future plans flexible so they can be adapted to changing circumstances.

# Recognizing moods of others

**1.** Notice the situation that is occurring.

**2.** Note the other person's facial expression, voice tone, and gestures.

**3.** Think about what feelings you are experiencing when you demonstrate similar behaviors.

**4.** Assess the other person's current mood or feelings.

**5.** If possible, check out your assessment with him or her.

# Resigning from a job or project

**1.** Find out the required amount of notice to be given.

**2.** Inform your supervisor calmly and pleasantly of your intention to resign.

**3.** Give a positive reason.

**4.** Always give at least the minimum amount of notice required.

**5.** Avoid walking off a job or leaving under negative circumstances.

# Resolving conflicts

**1.** Approach the situation calmly and rationally.

**2.** Listen to the other people involved.

**3.** Express your feelings appropriately and assertively.

**4.** Acknowledge other points of view.

**5.** Show that you are willing to negotiate and compromise.

**6.** Help arrive at a mutually beneficial resolution.

**7.** Thank the other person (or people) for cooperating.

# Rewarding yourself

**1.** Decide if what you have just done is praiseworthy.

**2.** If so, tell yourself you have done a good job and feel good about it.

**3.** Possibly give yourself an extra privilege or treat for a particular success.

**4.** Prompt yourself about your increasing competency and ability.

# Seeking professional assistance

**1.** Decide if you are having a serious problem or crisis.

**2.** Identify the type of professional that can help you.

**3.** Locate one through a referral from a professional you currently know or in the phone book.

**4.** Specifically describe your problem to the person you go to for help.

# Setting goals

1. Decide on your overall values and lifestyle desires.

2. List the resources you need to fulfill these lifestyle options.

3. Examine the intermediate steps in accomplishing your overall outcome.

4. Establish short- and long-term goals that will help you accomplish the steps necessary for the desired outcome.

# Stopping negative or harmful thoughts

**1.** Identify negative or repetitive thoughts you wish to avoid.

**2.** When these occur, consistently say to yourself, "Stop!"

**3.** Immediately visualize a more positive scene or relaxing thought.

**4.** Reward yourself for using strategies to stop your negative or harmful thoughts.

# Taking risks appropriately

**1.** Identify new activities that hold reasonable risks.

**2.** Evaluate whether these risks could be dangerous or have negative consequences.

**3.** If appropriate, try the new activity and do your best.

**4.** Ask for a trustworthy adult's advice if you are unsure.

## COMPLEX – SKILL 178
# Tolerating differences

**1.** Examine the similarities between you and another person.

**2.** Take note of the differences.

**3.** Emphasize the shared interests, tastes, and activities between you and the other person.

**4.** Express appreciation and respect for the other person as an individual.

# Using community resources

**1.** Identify your exact needs.

**2.** Use information numbers and phone directories to contact government agencies and services.

**3.** Use online search engines or phone directories to locate and contact nonprofit agencies that can assist you.

**4.** Look in the newspaper listings under "community services" for additional resources.

**5.** Ask staff members at public libraries for help in identifying community resources.

# Using leisure time

**1.** Engage in leisure activities when tasks are completed and with permission.

**2.** Choose activities that are age-appropriate, healthy, and productive.

**3.** Develop new interests and hobbies whenever possible.

**4.** Avoid delinquent or gang-related activities.

**5.** Limit your TV, computer, and videogame time.

**6.** Look at resources in the community for entertainment and fun.

# Using self-monitoring and self-reflection

**1.** Think about behaviors you are engaging in and the feelings you are having.

**2.** Correctly identify and label your behaviors and feelings.

**3.** Think about whether these are appropriate for the current situation.

**4.** Identify alternative behaviors or skills that would be more productive.

# Using strategies to find a job

**1.** Decide on the types of jobs you are qualified for.

**2.** Look in the newspaper or go online to check current employment ads.

**3.** Check the phone book for businesses where you can apply for a job. Start at their personnel offices.

**4.** Check with adults you know about businesses they may be familiar with.

**5.** Examine ads posted at local employment offices.

# Appendices

The following appendices are designed to serve as a guide for caregivers in identifying which skills to teach to the youth with whom they work.

Appendix A lists all skills in the Curriculum by skill type (social, emotional management, academic, moral/ethical, and independent living).

Appendix B groups skills by the character traits (trustworthiness, respect, responsibility, fairness, caring, and citizenship) the skills can be used to teach.

These groupings present the skills we suggest teaching in order to meet youth needs in specific skill areas, and the skills that can be taught to help develop and reinforce specific character traits.

Appendix C lists skills according to behavior problem areas. The problem areas are ones that we believe caregivers most commonly encounter in most child-care settings.

Appendix D categorizes skills by situations. These situation categories cover the most common areas where children need to use skills to function and succeed.

The categories provided in Appendices C and D are not comprehensive, and do not cover every possible scenario where skills should or must be taught to young people. The categories that are included were chosen because they represent the most common behavioral and situational areas we experience in our direct work with children and in the training and consultation we provide to child-care providers.

# APPENDIX A

# Social Skills Grouped by Skill Type

## Social

**Skill No.**     **Skill Name, Location**

1    Following Instructions, page 63

2    Accepting "No" for an Answer, page 65

3    Talking with Others, page 67

4    Introducing Yourself, page 69

5    Accepting Criticism or a Consequence, page 71

6    Disagreeing Appropriately, page 73

8    Showing Sensitivity to Others, page 79

9    Accepting Apologies from Others, page 81

10    Accepting Compliments, page 82

12    Accepting Decisions of Authority, page 84

13    Answering the Telephone, page 85

14    Asking for Clarification, page 87

15    Asking for Help, page 88

16    Asking Questions, page 89

18    Checking In (or Checking Back), page 91

19    Choosing Appropriate Words to Say, page 92

20    Closing a Conversation, page 93

23    Complying with Reasonable Requests, page 96

24    Contributing to Discussions (Joining in a Conversation), page 97

27    Following Rules, page 100

29    Getting Another Person's Attention, page 102

31    Giving Compliments, page 104

32    Greeting Others, page 105

33    Ignoring Distractions by Others, page 106

34    Initiating a Conversation, page 107

35    Interrupting Appropriately, page 108

36    Introducing Others, page 109

37    Listening to Others, page 110

38    Maintaining a Conversation, page 111

41    Making an Apology, page 114

42    Making a Request (Asking a Favor), page 115

| | | | | |
|---|---|---|---|---|
| 43 | Making a Telephone Call, page 116 | | 109 | Expressing Pride in Accomplishments, page 183 |
| 46 | Offering Assistance or Help, page 119 | | 111 | Following Through on Agreements and Contracts, page 185 |
| 47 | Participating in Activities, page 120 | | 112 | Giving Instructions, page 186 |
| 52 | Saying Good-Bye to Guests, page 125 | | 113 | Giving Rationales, page 187 |
| 53 | Saying "No" Assertively, page 126 | | 118 | Making New Friends, page 193 |
| 55 | Showing Appreciation, page 128 | | 121 | Negotiating with Others, page 196 |
| 56 | Showing Interest, page 129 | | 133 | Self-Correcting Own Behavior, page 208 |
| 57 | Staying on Task, page 130 | | 135 | Setting Appropriate Boundaries, page 210 |
| 59 | Using an Appropriate Voice Tone, page 132 | | 137 | Sharing Personal Experiences, page 212 |
| 61 | Using Structured Problem-Solving (SODAS), page 134 | | 138 | Suggesting an Activity, page 213 |
| 62 | Using Table Etiquette, page 135 | | 140 | Using Appropriate Language, page 215 |
| 63 | Volunteering, page 136 | | 148 | Asking for Advice, page 223 |
| 64 | Waiting Your Turn, page 137 | | 149 | Assessing Own Abilities, page 224 |
| 68 | Advocating for Oneself, page 141 | | 152 | Being Assertive, page 227 |
| 69 | Analyzing Skills Needed for Different Situations, page 142 | | 156 | Differentiating Friends from Acquaintances, page 231 |
| 70 | Analyzing Social Situations, page 143 | | 158 | Expressing Empathy and Understanding for Others, page 233 |
| 73 | Borrowing from Others, page 146 | | 165 | Maintaining Relationships, page 240 |
| 74 | Caring for Others' Property, page 147 | | 170 | Recognizing Moods of Others, page 245 |
| 77 | Choosing Appropriate Friends, page 150 | | | |

## Emotional Management

| **Skill No.** | **Skill Name, Location** |
|---|---|
| 80 | Compromising with Others, page 153 |
| 82 | Contributing to Group Activities, page 155 |
| 88 | Cooperating with Others, page 161 |
| 108 | Expressing Optimism, page 182 |
| 2 | Accepting "No" for an Answer, page 65 |
| 5 | Accepting Criticism or a Consequence, page 71 |

6    Disagreeing Appropriately, page 73

11   Accepting Consequences, page 83

19   Choosing Appropriate Words to Say, page 92

25   Correcting Another Person (or Giving Criticism), page 98

33   Ignoring Distractions by Others, page 106

44   Making Positive Self-Statements, page 117

45   Making Positive Statements about Others, page 118

54   Seeking Positive Attention, page 127

59   Using an Appropriate Voice Tone, page 132

60   Using Anger Control Strategies, page 133

64   Waiting Your Turn, page 137

65   Accepting Defeat or Loss, page 138

66   Accepting Help or Assistance, page 139

67   Accepting Winning Appropriately, page 140

70   Analyzing Social Situations, page 143

83   Controlling Eating Habits, page 156

84   Controlling Emotions, page 157

85   Controlling Sexually Abusive Impulses toward Others, page 158

86   Controlling the Impulse to Lie, page 159

87   Controlling the Impulse to Steal, page 160

89   Coping with Anger and Aggression from Others, page 162

90   Coping with Change, page 163

91   Coping with Conflict, page 164

92   Coping with Sad Feelings (or Depression), page 165

93   Dealing with an Accusation, page 166

94   Dealing with Being Left Out, page 168

95   Dealing with Boredom, page 169

96   Dealing with Contradictory Messages, page 170

97   Dealing with Embarrassing Situations, page 171

98   Dealing with Failure, page 172

99   Dealing with Fear, page 173

100  Dealing with Frustration, page 174

102  Dealing with Rejection, page 176

103  Delaying Gratification, page 177

105  Displaying Sportsmanship, page 179

106  Expressing Appropriate Affection, page 180

107  Expressing Feelings Appropriately, page 181

108  Expressing Optimism, page 182

109  Expressing Pride in Accomplishments, page 183

121  Negotiating with Others, page 196

125  Preparing for a Stressful Conversation, page 200

126  Preventing Trouble with Others, page 201

127    Problem-Solving a Disagreement, page 202

128    Responding to Complaints, page 203

129    Responding to Others' Feelings, page 204

130    Responding to Others' Humor, page 205

131    Responding to Teasing, page 206

133    Self-Correcting Own Behavior, page 208

134    Self-Reporting Own Behaviors, page 209

136    Sharing Attention with Others, page 211

141    Using Relaxation Strategies, page 216

142    Using Self-Talk or Self-Instruction, page 217

143    Using Spontaneous Problem-Solving, page 218

146    Accepting Self, page 221

147    Altering One's Environment, page 222

153    Being Patient, page 228

157    Displaying Appropriate Control, page 232

158    Expressing Empathy and Understanding for Others, page 233

159    Expressing Grief, page 234

162    Identifying Own Feelings, page 237

164    Laughing at Oneself, page 239

166    Making an Appropriate Complaint, page 241

168    Managing Stress, page 243

171    Resigning from a Job or Project, page 246

172    Resolving Conflicts, page 247

176    Stopping Negative or Harmful Thoughts, page 251

181    Using Self-Monitoring and Self-Reflection, page 256

# Ethical/Moral

| Skill No. | Skill Name, Location |
| --- | --- |
| 7 | Showing Respect, page 75 |
| 26 | Doing Good Quality Work, page 99 |
| 41 | Making an Apology, page 114 |
| 48 | Refraining from Possessing Contraband or Drugs, page 121 |
| 50 | Reporting Other Youths' Behavior (or Peer Reporting), page 123 |
| 51 | Resisting Peer Pressure, page 124 |
| 76 | Choosing Appropriate Clothing, page 149 |
| 78 | Communicating Honestly, page 151 |
| 101 | Dealing with Group Pressure, page 175 |
| 103 | Delaying Gratification, page 177 |
| 105 | Displaying Sportsmanship, page 179 |
| 106 | Expressing Appropriate Affection, page 180 |
| 114 | Interacting Appropriately with Members of the Opposite Sex, page 188 |
| 115 | Keeping Property in Its Place, page 190 |

| | |
|---|---|
| 116 | Lending to Others, page 191 |
| 119 | Making Restitution (Compensating), page 194 |
| 139 | Using Appropriate Humor, page 214 |
| 140 | Using Appropriate Language, page 215 |
| 150 | Being an Appropriate Role Model, page 225 |
| 155 | Clarifying Values and Beliefs, page 230 |
| 167 | Making Moral and Spiritual Decisions, page 242 |
| 177 | Taking Risks Appropriately, page 252 |
| 178 | Tolerating Differences, page 253 |

# Academic

| Skill No. | Skill Name, Location |
|---|---|
| 14 | Asking for Clarification, page 87 |
| 21 | Completing Homework, page 94 |
| 22 | Completing Tasks, page 95 |
| 30 | Getting the Teacher's Attention, page 103 |
| 57 | Staying on Task, page 130 |
| 72 | Being Prepared for Class, page 145 |
| 79 | Complying with School Dress Code, page 152 |
| 81 | Concentrating on a Subject or Task, page 154 |
| 104 | Displaying Effort, page 178 |
| 122 | Organizing Tasks and Activities, page 197 |
| 123 | Persevering on Tasks and Projects, page 198 |

| | |
|---|---|
| 132 | Responding to Written Requests, page 207 |
| 144 | Using Study Skills, page 219 |
| 145 | Working Independently, page 220 |
| 153 | Being Patient, page 228 |
| 161 | Gathering Information, page 236 |

# Independent Living

| Skill No. | Skill Name, Location |
|---|---|
| 13 | Answering the Telephone, page 85 |
| 17 | Being on Time (Promptness), page 90 |
| 26 | Doing Good Quality Work, page 99 |
| 28 | Following Written Instructions, page 101 |
| 39 | Maintaining an Appropriate Appearance, page 112 |
| 40 | Maintaining Personal Hygiene, page 113 |
| 47 | Participating in Activities, page 120 |
| 49 | Reporting Emergencies, page 122 |
| 58 | Trying New Tasks, page 131 |
| 61 | Using Structured Problem-Solving (SODAS), page 134 |
| 63 | Volunteering, page 136 |
| 71 | Analyzing Tasks to Be Completed, page 144 |
| 73 | Borrowing from Others, page 146 |
| 74 | Caring for Others' Property, page 147 |
| 75 | Caring for Own Belongings, page 148 |
| 76 | Choosing Appropriate Clothing, page 149 |

77    Choosing Appropriate Friends, page 150

83    Controlling Eating Habits, page 156

90    Coping with Change, page 163

104   Displaying Effort, page 178

110   Following Safety Rules, page 184

111   Following Through on Agreements and Contracts, page 185

112   Giving Instructions, page 186

117   Making Decisions, page 192

120   Managing Time, page 195

122   Organizing Tasks and Activities, page 197

123   Persevering on Tasks and Projects, page 198

124   Planning Meals, page 199

132   Responding to Written Requests, page 207

145   Working Independently, page 220

149   Assessing Own Abilities, page 224

151   Being a Consumer, page 226

154   Budgeting and Managing Money, page 229

160   Formulating Strategies, page 235

161   Gathering Information, page 236

163   Interviewing for a Job, page 238

169   Planning Ahead, page 244

171   Resigning from a Job or Project, page 246

173   Rewarding Yourself, page 248

174   Seeking Professional Assistance, page 249

175   Setting Goals, page 250

179   Using Community Resources, page 254

180   Using Leisure Time, page 255

182   Using Strategies to Find a Job, page 257

# APPENDIX B

# Social Skills Grouped by Character Trait

## Trustworthiness

| Skill No. | Skill Name, Location |
|---|---|
| 1 | Following Instructions, page 63 |
| 17 | Being on Time (Promptness), page 90 |
| 18 | Checking In (or Checking Back), page 91 |
| 23 | Complying with Reasonable Requests, page 96 |
| 27 | Following Rules, page 100 |
| 28 | Following Written Instructions, page 101 |
| 39 | Maintaining an Appropriate Appearance, page 112 |
| 48 | Refraining from Possessing Contraband or Drugs, page 121 |
| 50 | Reporting Other Youths' Behavior (or Peer Reporting), page 123 |
| 51 | Resisting Peer Pressure, page 124 |
| 57 | Staying on Task, page 130 |
| 58 | Trying New Tasks, page 131 |
| 68 | Advocating for Oneself, page 141 |
| 73 | Borrowing from Others, page 146 |
| 74 | Caring for Others' Property, page 147 |
| 77 | Choosing Appropriate Friends, page 150 |
| 78 | Communicating Honestly, page 151 |
| 86 | Controlling the Impulse to Lie, page 159 |
| 87 | Controlling the Impulse to Steal, page 160 |
| 95 | Dealing with Boredom, page 169 |
| 101 | Dealing with Group Pressure, page 175 |
| 104 | Displaying Effort, page 178 |
| 105 | Displaying Sportsmanship, page 179 |
| 108 | Expressing Optimism, page 182 |
| 109 | Expressing Pride in Accomplishments, page 183 |
| 111 | Following Through on Agreements and Contracts, page 185 |
| 115 | Keeping Property in Its Place, page 190 |
| 119 | Making Restitution (Compensating), page 194 |
| 120 | Managing Time, page 195 |
| 121 | Negotiating with Others, page 196 |

| | |
|---|---|
| 122 | Organizing Tasks and Activities, page 197 |
| 123 | Persevering on Tasks and Projects, page 198 |
| 131 | Responding to Teasing, page 206 |
| 132 | Responding to Written Requests, page 207 |
| 137 | Sharing Personal Experiences, page 212 |
| 145 | Working Independently, page 220 |
| 146 | Accepting Self, page 221 |
| 149 | Assessing Own Abilities, page 224 |
| 150 | Being an Appropriate Role Model, page 225 |
| 151 | Being a Consumer, page 226 |
| 154 | Budgeting and Managing Money, page 229 |
| 162 | Identifying Own Feelings, page 237 |
| 163 | Interviewing for a Job, page 238 |
| 167 | Making Moral and Spiritual Decisions, page 242 |
| 177 | Taking Risks Appropriately, page 252 |
| 179 | Using Community Resources, page 254 |
| 181 | Using Self-Monitoring and Self-Reflection, page 256 |

# Respect

| Skill No. | Skill Name, Location |
|---|---|
| 2 | Accepting "No" for an Answer, page 65 |
| 3 | Talking with Others, page 67 |
| 4 | Introducing Yourself, page 69 |
| 5 | Accepting Criticism or a Consequence, page 71 |
| 6 | Disagreeing Appropriately, page 73 |
| 7 | Showing Respect, page 75 |
| 8 | Showing Sensitivity to Others, page 79 |
| 9 | Accepting Apologies from Others, page 81 |
| 10 | Accepting Compliments, page 82 |
| 12 | Accepting Decisions of Authority, page 84 |
| 13 | Answering the Telephone, page 85 |
| 19 | Choosing Appropriate Words to Say, page 92 |
| 20 | Closing a Conversation, page 93 |
| 24 | Contributing to Discussions (Joining in a Conversation), page 97 |
| 25 | Correcting Another Person (or Giving Criticism), page 98 |
| 29 | Getting Another Person's Attention, page 102 |
| 30 | Getting the Teacher's Attention, page 103 |
| 32 | Greeting Others, page 105 |
| 33 | Ignoring Distractions by Others, page 106 |
| 34 | Initiating a Conversation, page 107 |
| 35 | Interrupting Appropriately, page 108 |
| 36 | Introducing Others, page 109 |
| 37 | Listening to Others, page 110 |
| 38 | Maintaining a Conversation, page 111 |

39   Maintaining an Appropriate
     Appearance, page 112

41   Making an Apology, page 114

42   Making a Request (Asking a
     Favor), page 115

44   Making Positive Self-Statements,
     page 117

45   Making Positive Statements about
     Others, page 118

52   Saying Good-Bye to Guests,
     page 125

53   Saying "No" Assertively, page 126

54   Seeking Positive Attention,
     page 127

55   Showing Appreciation, page 128

56   Showing Interest, page 129

59   Using an Appropriate Voice Tone,
     page 132

60   Using Anger Control Strategies,
     page 133

62   Using Table Etiquette, page 135

64   Waiting Your Turn, page 137

65   Accepting Defeat or Loss,
     page 138

66   Accepting Help or Assistance,
     page 139

67   Accepting Winning Appropriately,
     page 140

68   Advocating for Oneself, page 141

74   Caring for Others' Property,
     page 147

75   Caring for Own Belongings,
     page 148

76   Choosing Appropriate Clothing,
     page 149

77   Choosing Appropriate Friends,
     page 150

78   Communicating Honestly,
     page 151

80   Compromising with Others,
     page 153

84   Controlling Emotions, page 157

85   Controlling Sexually Abusive
     Impulses toward Others, page 158

87   Controlling the Impulse to Steal,
     page 160

89   Coping with Anger and
     Aggression from Others, page 162

91   Coping with Conflict, page 164

93   Dealing with an Accusation,
     page 166

94   Dealing with Being Left Out,
     page 168

97   Dealing with Embarrassing
     Situations, page 171

98   Dealing with Failure, page 172

99   Dealing with Fear, page 173

100  Dealing with Frustration, page 174

101  Dealing with Group Pressure,
     page 175

102  Dealing with Rejection, page 176

103  Delaying Gratification, page 177

105  Displaying Sportsmanship,
     page 179

106  Expressing Appropriate Affection,
     page 180

107  Expressing Feelings Appropriately,
     page 181

109  Expressing Pride in
     Accomplishments, page 183

112   Giving Instructions, page 186

113   Giving Rationales, page 187

114   Interacting Appropriately with Members of the Opposite Sex, page 188

115   Keeping Property in Its Place, page 190

118   Making New Friends, page 193

121   Negotiating with Others, page 196

125   Preparing for a Stressful Conversation, page 200

126   Preventing Trouble with Others, page 201

127   Problem-Solving a Disagreement, page 202

128   Responding to Complaints, page 203

129   Responding to Others' Feelings, page 204

130   Responding to Others' Humor, page 205

131   Responding to Teasing, page 206

133   Self-Correcting Own Behavior, page 208

134   Self-Reporting Own Behaviors, page 209

135   Setting Appropriate Boundaries, page 210

136   Sharing Attention with Others, page 211

137   Sharing Personal Experiences, page 212

139   Using Appropriate Humor, page 214

140   Using Appropriate Language, page 215

143   Using Spontaneous Problem-Solving, page 218

146   Accepting Self, page 221

148   Asking for Advice, page 223

150   Being an Appropriate Role Model, page 225

152   Being Assertive, page 227

153   Being Patient, page 228

155   Clarifying Values and Beliefs, page 230

156   Differentiating Friends from Acquaintances, page 231

157   Displaying Appropriate Control, page 232

158   Expressing Empathy and Understanding for Others, page 233

159   Expressing Grief, page 234

164   Laughing at Oneself, page 239

165   Maintaining Relationships, page 240

166   Making an Appropriate Complaint, page 241

167   Making Moral and Spiritual Decisions, page 242

170   Recognizing Moods of Others, page 245

172   Resolving Conflicts, page 247

176   Stopping Negative or Harmful Thoughts, page 251

178   Tolerating Differences, page 253

# Responsibility

Skill No.          Skill Name, Location

1         Following Instructions, page 63

2    Accepting "No" for an Answer, page 65

5    Accepting Criticism or a Consequence, page 71

6    Disagreeing Appropriately, page 73

11    Accepting Consequences, page 83

14    Asking for Clarification, page 87

15    Asking for Help, page 88

16    Asking Questions, page 89

17    Being on Time (Promptness), page 90

18    Checking In (or Checking Back), page 91

19    Choosing Appropriate Words to Say, page 92

21    Completing Homework, page 94

22    Completing Tasks, page 95

23    Complying with Reasonable Requests, page 96

26    Doing Good Quality Work, page 99

28    Following Written Instructions, page 101

33    Ignoring Distractions by Others, page 106

39    Maintaining an Appropriate Appearance, page 112

40    Maintaining Personal Hygiene, page 113

41    Making an Apology, page 114

48    Refraining from Possessing Contraband or Drugs, page 121

49    Reporting Emergencies, page 122

53    Saying "No" Assertively, page 126

57    Staying on Task, page 130

58    Trying New Tasks, page 131

60    Using Anger Control Strategies, page 133

61    Using Structured Problem-Solving (SODAS), page 134

63    Volunteering, page 136

68    Advocating for Oneself, page 141

69    Analyzing Skills Needed for Different Situations, page 142

70    Analyzing Social Situations, page 143

71    Analyzing Tasks to Be Completed, page 144

72    Being Prepared for Class, page 145

73    Borrowing from Others, page 146

75    Caring for Own Belongings, page 148

76    Choosing Appropriate Clothing, page 149

79    Complying with School Dress Code, page 152

81    Concentrating on a Subject or Task, page 154

82    Contributing to Group Activities, page 155

83    Controlling Eating Habits, page 156

84    Controlling Emotions, page 157

89    Coping with Anger and Aggression from Others, page 162

90    Coping with Change, page 163

91    Coping with Conflict, page 164

92    Coping with Sad Feelings (or Depression), page 165

| | | | |
|---|---|---|---|
| 93 | Dealing with an Accusation, page 166 | 127 | Problem-Solving a Disagreement, page 202 |
| 95 | Dealing with Boredom, page 169 | 132 | Responding to Written Requests, page 207 |
| 96 | Dealing with Contradictory Messages, page 170 | 133 | Self-Correcting Own Behavior, page 208 |
| 97 | Dealing with Embarrassing Situations, page 171 | 134 | Self-Reporting Own Behaviors, page 209 |
| 98 | Dealing with Failure, page 172 | 135 | Setting Appropriate Boundaries, page 210 |
| 99 | Dealing with Fear, page 173 | 139 | Using Appropriate Humor, page 214 |
| 100 | Dealing with Frustration, page 174 | 140 | Using Appropriate Language, page 215 |
| 104 | Displaying Effort, page 178 | 141 | Using Relaxation Strategies, page 216 |
| 105 | Displaying Sportsmanship, page 179 | 142 | Using Self-Talk or Self-Instruction, page 217 |
| 106 | Expressing Appropriate Affection, page 180 | 143 | Using Spontaneous Problem-Solving, page 218 |
| 108 | Expressing Optimism, page 182 | 144 | Using Study Skills, page 219 |
| 110 | Following Safety Rules, page 184 | 145 | Working Independently, page 220 |
| 111 | Following Through on Agreements and Contracts, page 185 | 147 | Altering One's Environment, page 222 |
| 114 | Interacting Appropriately with Members of the Opposite Sex, page 188 | 148 | Asking for Advice, page 223 |
| | | 149 | Assessing Own Abilities, page 224 |
| 115 | Keeping Property in Its Place, page 190 | 150 | Being an Appropriate Role Model, page 225 |
| 117 | Making Decisions, page 192 | 151 | Being a Consumer, page 226 |
| 119 | Making Restitution (Compensating), page 194 | 153 | Being Patient, page 228 |
| 120 | Managing Time, page 195 | 154 | Budgeting and Managing Money, page 229 |
| 122 | Organizing Tasks and Activities, page 197 | 156 | Differentiating Friends from Acquaintances, page 231 |
| 123 | Persevering on Tasks and Projects, page 198 | 157 | Displaying Appropriate Control, page 232 |
| 124 | Planning Meals, page 199 | | |
| 126 | Preventing Trouble with Others, page 201 | | |

160    Formulating Strategies, page 235

161    Gathering Information, page 236

162    Identifying Own Feelings, page 237

163    Interviewing for a Job, page 238

165    Maintaining Relationships, page 240

166    Making an Appropriate Complaint, page 241

168    Managing Stress, page 243

169    Planning Ahead, page 244

171    Resigning from a Job or Project, page 246

173    Rewarding Yourself, page 248

174    Seeking Professional Assistance, page 249

175    Setting Goals, page 250

176    Stopping Negative or Harmful Thoughts, page 251

177    Taking Risks Appropriately, page 252

180    Using Leisure Time, page 255

181    Using Self-Monitoring and Self-Reflection, page 256

182    Using Strategies to Find a Job, page 257

# Fairness

**Skill No.**    **Skill Name, Location**

37    Listening to Others, page 110

42    Making a Request (Asking a Favor), page 115

47    Participating in Activities, page 120

64    Waiting Your Turn, page 137

65    Accepting Defeat or Loss, page 138

66    Accepting Help or Assistance, page 139

67    Accepting Winning Appropriately, page 140

73    Borrowing from Others, page 146

80    Compromising with Others, page 153

93    Dealing with an Accusation, page 166

96    Dealing with Contradictory Messages, page 170

105    Displaying Sportsmanship, page 179

121    Negotiating with Others, page 196

123    Persevering on Tasks and Projects, page 198

125    Preparing for a Stressful Conversation, page 200

127    Problem-Solving a Disagreement, page 202

128    Responding to Complaints, page 203

129    Responding to Others' Feelings, page 204

134    Self-Reporting Own Behaviors, page 209

136    Sharing Attention with Others, page 211

138    Suggesting an Activity, page 213

150    Being an Appropriate Role Model, page 225

152    Being Assertive, page 227

155    Clarifying Values and Beliefs, page 230

164  Laughing at Oneself, page 239

172  Resolving Conflicts, page 247

178  Tolerating Differences, page 253

# Caring

**Skill No.**        **Skill Name, Location**

8  Showing Sensitivity to Others, page 79

9  Accepting Apologies from Others, page 81

10  Accepting Compliments, page 82

19  Choosing Appropriate Words to Say, page 92

25  Correcting Another Person (or Giving Criticism), page 98

31  Giving Compliments, page 104

44  Making Positive Self-Statements, page 117

45  Making Positive Statements about Others, page 118

46  Offering Assistance or Help, page 119

51  Resisting Peer Pressure, page 124

52  Saying Good-Bye to Guests, page 125

55  Showing Appreciation, page 128

56  Showing Interest, page 129

59  Using an Appropriate Voice Tone, page 132

85  Controlling Sexually Abusive Impulses toward Others, page 158

88  Cooperating with Others, page 161

89  Coping with Anger and Aggression from Others, page 162

94  Dealing with Being Left Out, page 168

103  Delaying Gratification, page 177

105  Displaying Sportsmanship, page 179

107  Expressing Feelings Appropriately, page 181

108  Expressing Optimism, page 182

109  Expressing Pride in Accomplishments, page 183

112  Giving Instructions, page 186

113  Giving Rationales, page 187

114  Interacting Appropriately with Members of the Opposite Sex, page 188

116  Lending to Others, page 191

118  Making New Friends, page 193

125  Preparing for a Stressful Conversation, page 200

129  Responding to Others' Feelings, page 204

131  Responding to Teasing, page 206

146  Accepting Self, page 221

150  Being an Appropriate Role Model, page 225

152  Being Assertive, page 227

155  Clarifying Values and Beliefs, page 230

157  Displaying Appropriate Control, page 232

158  Expressing Empathy and Understanding for Others, page 233

159  Expressing Grief, page 234

165  Maintaining Relationships, page 240

167  Making Moral and Spiritual Decisions, page 242

170   Recognizing Moods of Others, page 245

172   Resolving Conflicts, page 247

176   Stopping Negative or Harmful Thoughts, page 251

178   Tolerating Differences, page 253

# Citizenship

| Skill No. | Skill Name, Location |
| --- | --- |
| 3 | Talking with Others, page 67 |
| 4 | Introducing Yourself, page 69 |
| 7 | Showing Respect, page 75 |
| 11 | Accepting Consequences, page 83 |
| 12 | Accepting Decisions of Authority, page 84 |
| 23 | Complying with Reasonable Requests, page 96 |
| 24 | Contributing to Discussions (Joining in a Conversation), page 97 |
| 27 | Following Rules, page 100 |
| 30 | Getting the Teacher's Attention, page 103 |
| 32 | Greeting Others, page 105 |
| 43 | Making a Telephone Call, page 116 |
| 46 | Offering Assistance or Help, page 119 |
| 47 | Participating in Activities, page 120 |
| 48 | Refraining from Possessing Contraband or Drugs, page 121 |
| 49 | Reporting Emergencies, page 122 |
| 63 | Volunteering, page 136 |
| 65 | Accepting Defeat or Loss, page 138 |

| 67 | Accepting Winning Appropriately, page 140 |
| --- | --- |
| 79 | Complying with School Dress Code, page 152 |
| 82 | Contributing to Group Activities, page 155 |
| 88 | Cooperating with Others, page 161 |
| 90 | Coping with Change, page 163 |
| 103 | Delaying Gratification, page 177 |
| 104 | Displaying Effort, page 178 |
| 105 | Displaying Sportsmanship, page 179 |
| 110 | Following Safety Rules, page 184 |
| 111 | Following Through on Agreements and Contracts, page 185 |
| 116 | Lending to Others, page 191 |
| 126 | Preventing Trouble with Others, page 201 |
| 147 | Altering One's Environment, page 222 |
| 150 | Being an Appropriate Role Model, page 225 |
| 171 | Resigning from a Job or Project, page 246 |
| 178 | Tolerating Differences, page 253 |
| 179 | Using Community Resources, page 254 |
| 180 | Using Leisure Time, page 255 |

# APPENDIX C

# Social Skills Grouped by Behavior Problems

## Aggressive and antisocial behavior

| Skill No. | Skill Name, Location |
|---|---|
| 1 | Following Instructions, page 63 |
| 2 | Accepting "No" for an Answer, page 65 |
| 5 | Accepting Criticism or a Consequence, page 71 |
| 6 | Disagreeing Appropriately, page 73 |
| 8 | Showing Sensitivity to Others, page 79 |
| 11 | Accepting Consequences, page 83 |
| 14 | Asking for Clarification, page 87 |
| 15 | Asking for Help, page 88 |
| 25 | Correcting Another Person (or Giving Criticism), page 98 |
| 27 | Following Rules, page 100 |
| 35 | Interrupting Appropriately, page 108 |
| 37 | Listening to Others, page 110 |
| 41 | Making an Apology, page 114 |
| 45 | Making Positive Statements about Others, page 118 |
| 51 | Resisting Peer Pressure, page 124 |
| 59 | Using an Appropriate Voice Tone, page 132 |
| 60 | Using Anger Control Strategies, page 133 |
| 61 | Using Structured Problem-Solving (SODAS), page 134 |
| 69 | Analyzing Skills Needed for Different Situations, page 142 |
| 80 | Compromising with Others, page 153 |
| 84 | Controlling Emotions, page 157 |
| 89 | Coping with Anger and Aggression from Others, page 162 |
| 93 | Dealing with an Accusation, page 166 |
| 100 | Dealing with Frustration, page 174 |
| 101 | Dealing with Group Pressure, page 175 |
| 107 | Expressing Feelings Appropriately, page 181 |
| 119 | Making Restitution (Compensating), page 194 |
| 121 | Negotiating with Others, page 196 |
| 125 | Preparing for a Stressful Conversation, page 200 |
| 127 | Problem-Solving a Disagreement, page 202 |

133    Self-Correcting Own Behavior, page 208

141    Using Relaxation Strategies, page 216

143    Using Spontaneous Problem-Solving, page 218

152    Being Assertive, page 227

157    Displaying Appropriate Control, page 232

158    Expressing Empathy and Understanding for Others, page 233

164    Laughing at Oneself, page 239

166    Making an Appropriate Complaint, page 241

168    Managing Stress, page 243

172    Resolving Conflicts, page 247

181    Using Self-Monitoring and Self-Reflection, page 256

# Depression and withdrawal problems

**Skill No.**        **Skill Name, Location**

3    Talking with Others, page 67

4    Introducing Yourself, page 69

6    Disagreeing Appropriately, page 73

10    Accepting Compliments, page 82

15    Asking for Help, page 88

18    Checking In (or Checking Back), page 91

20    Closing a Conversation, page 93

22    Completing Tasks, page 95

24    Contributing to Discussions (Joining in a Conversation), page 97

31    Giving Compliments, page 104

32    Greeting Others, page 105

34    Initiating a Conversation, page 107

38    Maintaining a Conversation, page 111

39    Maintaining an Appropriate Appearance, page 112

40    Maintaining Personal Hygiene, page 113

44    Making Positive Self-Statements, page 117

45    Making Positive Statements about Others, page 118

47    Participating in Activities, page 120

51    Resisting Peer Pressure, page 124

53    Saying "No" Assertively, page 126

54    Seeking Positive Attention, page 127

58    Trying New Tasks, page 131

59    Using an Appropriate Voice Tone, page 132

61    Using Structured Problem-Solving (SODAS), page 134

66    Accepting Help or Assistance, page 139

69    Analyzing Skills Needed for Different Situations, page 142

83    Controlling Eating Habits, page 156

90    Coping with Change, page 163

92    Coping with Sad Feelings (or Depression), page 165

95    Dealing with Boredom, page 169

98    Dealing with Failure, page 172

102    Dealing with Rejection, page 176

108    Expressing Optimism, page 182

109    Expressing Pride in Accomplishments, page 183

117    Making Decisions, page 192

118    Making New Friends, page 193

134    Self-Reporting Own Behaviors, page 209

143    Using Spontaneous Problem-Solving, page 218

148    Asking for Advice, page 223

152    Being Assertive, page 227

166    Making an Appropriate Complaint, page 241

168    Managing Stress, page 243

172    Resolving Conflicts, page 247

# Serious conflicts with authority figures

| Skill No. | Skill Name, Location |
| --- | --- |
| 1 | Following Instructions, page 63 |
| 2 | Accepting "No" for an Answer, page 65 |
| 3 | Talking with Others, page 67 |
| 4 | Introducing Yourself, page 69 |
| 5 | Accepting Criticism or a Consequence, page 71 |
| 6 | Disagreeing Appropriately, page 73 |
| 11 | Accepting Consequences, page 83 |
| 12 | Accepting Decisions of Authority, page 84 |
| 14 | Asking for Clarification, page 87 |
| 15 | Asking for Help, page 88 |

| 17 | Being on Time (Promptness), page 90 |
| 23 | Complying with Reasonable Requests, page 96 |
| 27 | Following Rules, page 100 |
| 35 | Interrupting Appropriately, page 108 |
| 37 | Listening to Others, page 110 |
| 41 | Making an Apology, page 114 |
| 50 | Reporting Other Youths' Behavior (or Peer Reporting), page 123 |
| 54 | Seeking Positive Attention, page 127 |
| 59 | Using an Appropriate Voice Tone, page 132 |
| 60 | Using Anger Control Strategies, page 133 |
| 61 | Using Structured Problem-Solving (SODAS), page 134 |
| 63 | Volunteering, page 136 |
| 69 | Analyzing Skills Needed for Different Situations, page 142 |
| 78 | Communicating Honestly, page 151 |
| 86 | Controlling the Impulse to Lie, page 159 |
| 93 | Dealing with an Accusation, page 166 |
| 105 | Displaying Sportsmanship, page 179 |
| 111 | Following Through on Agreements and Contracts, page 185 |
| 115 | Keeping Property in Its Place, page 190 |
| 125 | Preparing for a Stressful Conversation, page 200 |

| 127 | Problem-Solving a Disagreement, page 202 |
| 132 | Responding to Written Requests, page 207 |
| 134 | Self-Reporting Own Behaviors, page 209 |
| 143 | Using Spontaneous Problem-Solving, page 218 |
| 148 | Asking for Advice, page 223 |
| 152 | Being Assertive, page 227 |
| 166 | Making an Appropriate Complaint, page 241 |
| 168 | Managing Stress, page 243 |
| 172 | Resolving Conflicts, page 247 |
| 176 | Stopping Negative or Harmful Thoughts, page 251 |

# Sexual behavior or identity problems

| Skill No. | Skill Name, Location |
| --- | --- |
| 2 | Accepting "No" for an Answer, page 65 |
| 5 | Accepting Criticism or a Consequence, page 71 |
| 8 | Showing Sensitivity to Others, page 79 |
| 12 | Accepting Decisions of Authority, page 84 |
| 15 | Asking for Help, page 88 |
| 18 | Checking In (or Checking Back), page 91 |
| 19 | Choosing Appropriate Words to Say, page 92 |
| 27 | Following Rules, page 100 |
| 33 | Ignoring Distractions by Others, page 106 |
| 39 | Maintaining an Appropriate Appearance, page 112 |
| 40 | Maintaining Personal Hygiene, page 113 |
| 41 | Making an Apology, page 114 |
| 44 | Making Positive Self-Statements, page 117 |
| 50 | Reporting Other Youths' Behavior (or Peer Reporting), page 123 |
| 51 | Resisting Peer Pressure, page 124 |
| 53 | Saying "No" Assertively, page 126 |
| 54 | Seeking Positive Attention, page 127 |
| 59 | Using an Appropriate Voice Tone, page 132 |
| 61 | Using Structured Problem-Solving (SODAS), page 134 |
| 70 | Analyzing Social Situations, page 143 |
| 76 | Choosing Appropriate Clothing, page 149 |
| 77 | Choosing Appropriate Friends, page 150 |
| 78 | Communicating Honestly, page 151 |
| 79 | Complying with School Dress Code, page 152 |
| 84 | Controlling Emotions, page 157 |
| 85 | Controlling Sexually Abusive Impulses toward Others, page 158 |
| 92 | Coping with Sad Feelings (or Depression), page 165 |
| 95 | Dealing with Boredom, page 169 |
| 97 | Dealing with Embarrassing Situations, page 171 |
| 103 | Delaying Gratification, page 177 |

105    Displaying Sportsmanship, page 179

106    Expressing Appropriate Affection, page 180

107    Expressing Feelings Appropriately, page 181

114    Interacting Appropriately with Members of the Opposite Sex, page 188

117    Making Decisions, page 192

118    Making New Friends, page 193

133    Self-Correcting Own Behavior, page 208

134    Self-Reporting Own Behaviors, page 209

135    Setting Appropriate Boundaries, page 210

137    Sharing Personal Experiences, page 212

140    Using Appropriate Language, page 215

142    Using Self-Talk or Self-Instruction, page 217

143    Using Spontaneous Problem-Solving, page 218

146    Accepting Self, page 221

155    Clarifying Values and Beliefs, page 230

156    Differentiating Friends from Acquaintances, page 231

157    Displaying Appropriate Control, page 232

162    Identifying Own Feelings, page 237

167    Making Moral and Spiritual Decisions, page 242

174    Seeking Professional Assistance, page 249

180    Using Leisure Time, page 255

181    Using Self-Monitoring and Self-Reflection, page 256

# Sexual perpetrator behavior

| Skill No. | Skill Name, Location |
| --- | --- |
| 2 | Accepting "No" for an Answer, page 65 |
| 5 | Accepting Criticism or a Consequence, page 71 |
| 7 | Showing Respect, page 75 |
| 8 | Showing Sensitivity to Others, page 79 |
| 11 | Accepting Consequences, page 83 |
| 15 | Asking for Help, page 88 |
| 18 | Checking In (or Checking Back), page 91 |
| 41 | Making an Apology, page 114 |
| 42 | Making a Request (Asking a Favor), page 115 |
| 45 | Making Positive Statements about Others, page 118 |
| 50 | Reporting Other Youths' Behavior (or Peer Reporting), page 123 |
| 54 | Seeking Positive Attention, page 127 |
| 60 | Using Anger Control Strategies, page 133 |
| 61 | Using Structured Problem-Solving (SODAS), page 134 |
| 65 | Accepting Defeat or Loss, page 138 |

70   Analyzing Social Situations, page 143

77   Choosing Appropriate Friends, page 150

78   Communicating Honestly, page 151

84   Controlling Emotions, page 157

85   Controlling Sexually Abusive Impulses toward Others, page 158

86   Controlling the Impulse to Lie, page 159

95   Dealing with Boredom, page 169

100   Dealing with Frustration, page 174

102   Dealing with Rejection, page 176

103   Delaying Gratification, page 177

106   Expressing Appropriate Affection, page 180

113   Giving Rationals, page 187

114   Interacting Appropriately with Members of the Opposite Sex, page 188

117   Making Decisions, page 192

119   Making Restitution (Compensating), page 194

125   Preparing for a Stressful Conversation, page 200

133   Self-Correcting Own Behavior, page 208

134   Self-Reporting Own Behaviors, page 209

135   Setting Appropriate Boundaries, page 210

137   Sharing Personal Experiences, page 212

140   Using Appropriate Language, page 215

141   Using Relaxation Strategies, page 216

142   Using Self-Talk or Self-Instruction, page 217

143   Using Spontaneous Problem-Solving, page 218

150   Being an Appropriate Role Model, page 225

155   Clarifying Values and Beliefs, page 230

157   Displaying Appropriate Control, page 232

158   Expressing Empathy and Understanding for Others, page 233

162   Identifying Own Feelings, page 237

165   Maintaining Relationships, page 240

167   Making Moral and Spiritual Decisions, page 242

168   Managing Stress, page 243

174   Seeking Professional Assistance, page 249

176   Stopping Negative or Harmful Thoughts, page 251

180   Using Leisure Time, page 255

181   Using Self-Monitoring and Self-Reflection, page 256

# Peer interaction problems

| Skill No. | Skill Name, Location |
| --- | --- |
| 2 | Accepting "No" for an Answer, page 65 |
| 3 | Talking with Others, page 67 |
| 4 | Introducing Yourself, page 69 |

5   Accepting Criticism or a
    Consequence, page 71

6   Disagreeing Appropriately,
    page 73

8   Showing Sensitivity to Others,
    page 79

9   Accepting Apologies from Others,
    page 81

10  Accepting Compliments, page 82

19  Choosing Appropriate Words to
    Say, page 92

24  Contributing to Discussions
    (Joining in a Conversation),
    page 97

25  Correcting Another Person (or
    Giving Criticism), page 98

29  Getting Another Person's
    Attention, page 102

31  Giving Compliments, page 104

33  Ignoring Distractions by Others,
    page 106

37  Listening to Others, page 110

40  Maintaining Personal Hygiene,
    page 113

41  Making an Apology, page 114

47  Participating in Activities,
    page 120

48  Refraining from Possessing
    Contraband or Drugs, page 121

50  Reporting Other Youths' Behavior
    (or Peer Reporting), page 123

51  Resisting Peer Pressure, page 124

53  Saying "No" Assertively, page 126

59  Using an Appropriate Voice Tone,
    page 132

64  Waiting Your Turn, page 137

65  Accepting Defeat or Loss,
    page 138

67  Accepting Winning Appropriately,
    page 140

69  Analyzing Skills Needed for
    Different Situations, page 142

73  Borrowing from Others, page 146

74  Caring for Others' Property,
    page 147

77  Choosing Appropriate Friends,
    page 150

80  Compromising with Others,
    page 153

82  Contributing to Group Activities,
    page 155

89  Coping with Anger and
    Aggression from Others, page 162

94  Dealing with Being Left Out,
    page 168

97  Dealing with Embarrassing
    Situations, page 171

101 Dealing with Group Pressure,
    page 175

105 Displaying Sportsmanship,
    page 179

114 Interacting Appropriately with
    Members of the Opposite Sex,
    page 188

121 Negotiating with Others, page 196

127 Problem-Solving a Disagreement,
    page 202

129 Responding to Others' Feelings,
    page 204

131 Responding to Teasing, page 206

136 Sharing Attention with Others,
    page 211

| 150 | Being an Appropriate Role Model, page 225 |
| 152 | Being Assertive, page 227 |
| 164 | Laughing at Oneself, page 239 |
| 165 | Maintaining Relationships, page 240 |
| 178 | Tolerating Differences, page 253 |
| 180 | Using Leisure Time, page 255 |

# School behavior and attendance problems

| Skill No. | Skill Name, Location |
| --- | --- |
| 1 | Following Instructions, page 63 |
| 5 | Accepting Criticism or a Consequence, page 71 |
| 11 | Accepting Consequences, page 83 |
| 12 | Accepting Decisions of Authority, page 84 |
| 15 | Asking for Help, page 88 |
| 17 | Being on Time (Promptness), page 90 |
| 21 | Completing Homework, page 94 |
| 23 | Complying with Reasonable Requests, page 96 |
| 26 | Doing Good Quality Work, page 99 |
| 27 | Following Rules, page 100 |
| 28 | Following Written Instructions, page 101 |
| 30 | Getting the Teacher's Attention, page 103 |
| 33 | Ignoring Distractions by Others, page 106 |
| 35 | Interrupting Appropriately, page 108 |
| 37 | Listening to Others, page 110 |
| 39 | Maintaining an Appropriate Appearance, page 112 |
| 41 | Making an Apology, page 114 |
| 47 | Participating in Activities, page 120 |
| 54 | Seeking Positive Attention, page 127 |
| 57 | Staying on Task, page 130 |
| 63 | Volunteering, page 136 |
| 64 | Waiting Your Turn, page 137 |
| 66 | Accepting Help or Assistance, page 139 |
| 67 | Accepting Winning Appropriately, page 140 |
| 72 | Being Prepared for Class, page 145 |
| 75 | Caring for Own Belongings, page 148 |
| 78 | Communicating Honestly, page 151 |
| 79 | Complying with School Dress Code, page 152 |
| 81 | Concentrating on a Subject or Task, page 154 |
| 82 | Contributing to Group Activities, page 155 |
| 89 | Coping with Anger and Aggression from Others, page 162 |
| 93 | Dealing with an Accusation, page 166 |
| 97 | Dealing with Embarrassing Situations, page 171 |

101 Dealing with Group Pressure, page 175

109 Expressing Pride in Accomplishments, page 183

120 Managing Time, page 195

122 Organizing Tasks and Activities, page 197

123 Persevering on Tasks and Projects, page 198

127 Problem-Solving a Disagreement, page 202

131 Responding to Teasing, page 206

132 Responding to Written Requests, page 207

133 Self-Correcting Own Behavior, page 208

136 Sharing Attention with Others, page 211

142 Using Self-Talk or Self-Instruction, page 217

143 Using Spontaneous Problem-Solving, page 218

144 Using Study Skills, page 219

145 Working Independently, page 220

148 Asking for Advice, page 223

161 Gathering Information, page 236

175 Setting Goals, page 250

# Dishonesty or stealing behavior

| Skill No. | Skill Name, Location |
| --- | --- |
| 1 | Following Instructions, page 63 |
| 2 | Accepting "No" for an Answer, page 65 |
| 7 | Showing Respect, page 75 |
| 8 | Showing Sensitivity to Others, page 79 |
| 11 | Accepting Consequences, page 83 |
| 12 | Accepting Decisions of Authority, page 84 |
| 14 | Asking for Clarification, page 87 |
| 17 | Being on Time (Promptness), page 90 |
| 18 | Checking In (or Checking Back), page 91 |
| 27 | Following Rules, page 100 |
| 41 | Making an Apology, page 114 |
| 48 | Refraining from Possessing Contraband or Drugs, page 121 |
| 50 | Reporting Other Youths' Behavior (or Peer Reporting), page 123 |
| 51 | Resisting Peer Pressure, page 124 |
| 59 | Using an Appropriate Voice Tone, page 132 |
| 61 | Using Structured Problem-Solving (SODAS), page 134 |
| 73 | Borrowing from Others, page 146 |
| 74 | Caring for Others' Property, page 147 |
| 77 | Choosing Appropriate Friends, page 150 |
| 78 | Communicating Honestly, page 151 |
| 86 | Controlling the Impulse to Lie, page 159 |
| 87 | Controlling the Impulse to Steal, page 160 |
| 93 | Dealing with an Accusation, page 166 |

95    Dealing with Boredom, page 169

96    Dealing with Contradictory Messages, page 170

101   Dealing with Group Pressure, page 175

103   Delaying Gratification, page 177

111   Following Through on Agreements and Contracts, page 185

115   Keeping Property in Its Place, page 190

116   Lending to Others, page 191

119   Making Restitution (Compensating), page 194

133   Self-Correcting Own Behavior, page 208

134   Self-Reporting Own Behaviors, page 209

143   Using Spontaneous Problem-Solving, page 218

147   Altering One's Environment, page 222

153   Being Patient, page 228

154   Budgeting and Managing Money, page 229

155   Clarifying Values and Beliefs, page 230

167   Making Moral and Spiritual Decisions, page 242

169   Planning Ahead, page 244

175   Setting Goals, page 250

180   Using Leisure Time, page 255

# Impulse control difficulty and attention deficits

**Skill No.**        **Skill Name, Location**

1     Following Instructions, page 63

2     Accepting "No" for an Answer, page 65

5     Accepting Criticism or a Consequence, page 71

21    Completing Homework, page 94

22    Completing Tasks, page 95

24    Contributing to Discussions (Joining in a Conversation), page 97

26    Doing Good Quality Work, page 99

29    Getting Another Person's Attention, page 102

30    Getting the Teacher's Attention, page 103

33    Ignoring Distractions by Others, page 106

37    Listening to Others, page 110

42    Making a Request (Asking a Favor), page 115

47    Participating in Activities, page 120

51    Resisting Peer Pressure, page 124

54    Seeking Positive Attention, page 127

57    Staying on Task, page 130

59    Using an Appropriate Voice Tone, page 132

64    Waiting Your Turn, page 137

66    Accepting Help or Assistance, page 139

69    Analyzing Skills Needed for Different Situations, page 142

71    Analyzing Tasks to Be Completed, page 144

81    Concentrating on a Subject or Task, page 154

| 95 | Dealing with Boredom, page 169 |
|---|---|
| 100 | Dealing with Frustration, page 174 |
| 103 | Delaying Gratification, page 177 |
| 120 | Managing Time, page 195 |
| 122 | Organizing Tasks and Activities, page 197 |
| 123 | Persevering on Tasks and Projects, page 198 |
| 131 | Responding to Teasing, page 206 |
| 133 | Self-Correcting Own Behavior, page 208 |
| 136 | Sharing Attention with Others, page 211 |
| 139 | Using Appropriate Humor, page 214 |
| 140 | Using Appropriate Language, page 215 |
| 141 | Using Relaxation Strategies, page 216 |
| 142 | Using Self-Talk or Self-Instruction, page 217 |
| 143 | Using Spontaneous Problem-Solving, page 218 |
| 144 | Using Study Skills, page 219 |
| 145 | Working Independently, page 220 |
| 153 | Being Patient, page 228 |
| 157 | Displaying Appropriate Control, page 232 |
| 160 | Formulating Strategies, page 235 |
| 168 | Managing Stress, page 243 |
| 169 | Planning Ahead, page 244 |
| 175 | Setting Goals, page 250 |
| 176 | Stopping Negative or Harmful Thoughts, page 251 |
| 181 | Using Self-Monitoring and Self-Reflection, page 256 |

# Chronic relocation and running away

| Skill No. | Skill Name, Location |
|---|---|
| 2 | Accepting "No" for an Answer, page 65 |
| 3 | Talking with Others, page 67 |
| 5 | Accepting Criticism or a Consequence, page 71 |
| 6 | Disagreeing Appropriately, page 73 |
| 11 | Accepting Consequences, page 83 |
| 12 | Accepting Decisions of Authority, page 84 |
| 13 | Answering the Telephone, page 85 |
| 15 | Asking for Help, page 88 |
| 17 | Being on Time (Promptness), page 90 |
| 18 | Checking In (or Checking Back), page 91 |
| 23 | Complying with Reasonable Requests, page 96 |
| 27 | Following Rules, page 100 |
| 44 | Making Positive Self-Statements, page 117 |
| 45 | Making Positive Statements about Others, page 118 |
| 47 | Participating in Activities, page 120 |
| 48 | Refraining from Possessing Contraband or Drugs, page 121 |
| 50 | Reporting Other Youths' Behavior (or Peer Reporting), page 123 |
| 51 | Resisting Peer Pressure, page 124 |

53     Saying "No" Assertively, page 126

61     Using Structured Problem-Solving (SODAS), page 134

65     Accepting Defeat or Loss, page 138

66     Accepting Help or Assistance, page 139

69     Analyzing Skills Needed for Different Situations, page 142

78     Communicating Honestly, page 151

80     Compromising with Others, page 153

84     Controlling Emotions, page 157

86     Controlling the Impulse to Lie, page 159

89     Coping with Anger and Aggression from Others, page 162

90     Coping with Change, page 163

91     Coping with Conflict, page 164

92     Coping with Sad Feelings (or Depression), page 165

93     Dealing with an Accusation, page 166

98     Dealing with Failure, page 172

101    Dealing with Group Pressure, page 175

103    Delaying Gratification, page 177

117    Making Decisions, page 192

125    Preparing for a Stressful Conversation, page 200

126    Preventing Trouble with Others, page 201

127    Problem-Solving a Disagreement, page 202

131    Responding to Teasing, page 206

134    Self-Reporting Own Behaviors, page 209

141    Using Relaxation Strategies, page 216

142    Using Self-Talk or Self-Instruction, page 217

143    Using Spontaneous Problem-Solving, page 218

147    Altering One's Environment, page 222

157    Displaying Appropriate Control, page 232

159    Expressing Grief, page 234

162    Identifying Own Feelings, page 237

166    Making an Appropriate Complaint, page 241

168    Managing Stress, page 243

172    Resolving Conflicts, page 247

174    Seeking Professional Assistance, page 249

180    Using Leisure Time, page 255

181    Using Self-Monitoring and Self-Reflection, page 256

# Low self-esteem

**Skill No.**        **Skill Name, Location**

3     Talking with Others, page 67

4     Introducing Yourself, page 69

5     Accepting Criticism or a Consequence, page 71

9     Accepting Apologies from Others, page 81

10    Accepting Compliments, page 82

15    Asking for Help, page 88

16    Asking Questions, page 89

| | | | | |
|---|---|---|---|---|
| 20 | Closing a Conversation, page 93 | | 76 | Choosing Appropriate Clothing, page 149 |
| 24 | Contributing to Discussions (Joining in a Conversation), page 97 | | 82 | Contributing to Group Activities, page 155 |
| 25 | Correcting Another Person (or Giving Criticism), page 98 | | 83 | Controlling Eating Habits, page 156 |
| 26 | Doing Good Quality Work, page 99 | | 90 | Coping with Change, page 163 |
| 31 | Giving Compliments, page 104 | | 92 | Coping with Sad Feelings (or Depression), page 165 |
| 34 | Initiating a Conversation, page 107 | | 94 | Dealing with Being Left Out, page 168 |
| 38 | Maintaining a Conversation, page 111 | | 98 | Dealing with Failure, page 172 |
| 39 | Maintaining an Appropriate Appearance, page 112 | | 99 | Dealing with Fear, page 173 |
| 40 | Maintaining Personal Hygiene, page 113 | | 107 | Expressing Feelings Appropriately, page 181 |
| 44 | Making Positive Self-Statements, page 117 | | 109 | Expressing Pride in Accomplishments, page 183 |
| 45 | Making Positive Statements about Others, page 118 | | 117 | Making Decisions, page 192 |
| 47 | Participating in Activities, page 120 | | 118 | Making New Friends, page 193 |
| 58 | Trying New Tasks, page 131 | | 123 | Persevering on Tasks and Projects, page 198 |
| 59 | Using an Appropriate Voice Tone, page 132 | | 142 | Using Self-Talk or Self-Instruction, page 217 |
| 62 | Using Table Etiquette, page 135 | | 146 | Accepting Self, page 221 |
| 65 | Accepting Defeat or Loss, page 138 | | 149 | Assessing Own Abilities, page 224 |
| 66 | Accepting Help or Assistance, page 139 | | 152 | Being Assertive, page 227 |
| 67 | Accepting Winning Appropriately, page 140 | | 162 | Identifying Own Feelings, page 237 |
| 68 | Advocating for Oneself, page 141 | | 164 | Laughing at Oneself, page 239 |
| 75 | Caring for Own Belongings, page 148 | | 173 | Rewarding Yourself, page 248 |
| | | | 174 | Seeking Professional Assistance, page 249 |

| 177 | Taking Risks Appropriately, page 252 |
| 180 | Using Leisure Time, page 255 |

# Drug and alcohol abuse

| Skill No. | Skill Name, Location |
|---|---|
| 1 | Following Instructions, page 63 |
| 11 | Accepting Consequences, page 83 |
| 12 | Accepting Decisions of Authority, page 84 |
| 15 | Asking for Help, page 88 |
| 17 | Being on Time (Promptness), page 90 |
| 19 | Choosing Appropriate Words to Say, page 92 |
| 27 | Following Rules, page 100 |
| 37 | Listening to Others, page 110 |
| 39 | Maintaining an Appropriate Appearance, page 112 |
| 41 | Making an Apology, page 114 |
| 47 | Participating in Activities, page 120 |
| 48 | Refraining from Possessing Contraband or Drugs, page 121 |
| 50 | Reporting Other Youths' Behavior (or Peer Reporting), page 123 |
| 51 | Resisting Peer Pressure, page 124 |
| 53 | Saying "No" Assertively, page 126 |
| 54 | Seeking Positive Attention, page 127 |
| 61 | Using Structured Problem-Solving (SODAS), page 134 |
| 66 | Accepting Help or Assistance, page 139 |
| 73 | Borrowing from Others, page 146 |
| 76 | Choosing Appropriate Clothing, page 149 |
| 77 | Choosing Appropriate Friends, page 150 |
| 78 | Communicating Honestly, page 151 |
| 79 | Complying with School Dress Code, page 152 |
| 86 | Controlling the Impulse to Lie, page 159 |
| 87 | Controlling the Impulse to Steal, page 160 |
| 95 | Dealing with Boredom, page 169 |
| 101 | Dealing with Group Pressure, page 175 |
| 103 | Delaying Gratification, page 177 |
| 105 | Displaying Sportsmanship, page 179 |
| 107 | Expressing Feelings Appropriately, page 181 |
| 111 | Following Through on Agreements and Contracts, page 185 |
| 115 | Keeping Property in Its Place, page 190 |
| 116 | Lending to Others, page 191 |
| 117 | Making Decisions, page 192 |
| 119 | Making Restitution (Compensating), page 194 |
| 120 | Managing Time, page 195 |
| 134 | Self-Reporting Own Behaviors, page 209 |
| 141 | Using Relaxation Strategies, page 216 |
| 147 | Altering One's Environment, page 222 |
| 150 | Being an Appropriate Role Model, page 225 |

155    Clarifying Values and Beliefs,
       page 230

157    Displaying Appropriate Control,
       page 232

162    Identifying Own Feelings,
       page 237

167    Making Moral and Spiritual
       Decisions, page 242

168    Managing Stress, page 243

174    Seeking Professional Assistance,
       page 249

179    Using Community Resources,
       page 254

180    Using Leisure Time, page 255

181    Using Self-Monitoring and Self-
       Reflection, page 256

# APPENDIX D

# Social Skills Grouped by Situation

## Interactions with parents and family

**Skill No.**      **Skill Name, Location**

1    Following Instructions, page 63

2    Accepting "No" for an Answer, page 65

3    Talking with Others, page 67

5    Accepting Criticism or a Consequence, page 71

6    Disagreeing Appropriately, page 73

7    Showing Respect, page 75

9    Accepting Apologies from Others, page 81

10    Accepting Compliments, page 82

11    Accepting Consequences, page 83

13    Answering the Telephone, page 85

18    Checking In (or Checking Back), page 91

22    Completing Tasks, page 95

25    Correcting Another Person (or Giving Criticism), page 98

27    Following Rules, page 100

31    Giving Compliments, page 104

34    Initiating a Conversation, page 107

37    Listening to Others, page 110

41    Making an Apology, page 114

43    Making a Telephone Call, page 116

49    Reporting Emergencies, page 122

52    Saying Good-Bye to Guests, page 125

54    Seeking Positive Attention, page 127

55    Showing Appreciation, page 128

62    Using Table Etiquette, page 135

66    Accepting Help or Assistance, page 139

71    Analyzing Tasks to Be Completed, page 144

74    Caring for Others' Property, page 147

75    Caring for Own Belongings, page 148

76    Choosing Appropriate Clothing, page 149

78    Communicating Honestly, page 151

80    Compromising with Others, page 153

84    Controlling Emotions, page 157

85    Controlling Sexually Abusive Impulses toward Others, page 158

86    Controlling the Impulse to Lie, page 159

87    Controlling the Impulse to Steal, page 160

89    Coping with Anger and Aggression from Others, page 162

93    Dealing with an Accusation, page 166

106    Expressing Appropriate Affection, page 180

107    Expressing Feelings Appropriately, page 181

110    Following Safety Rules, page 184

111    Following Through on Agreements and Contracts, page 185

112    Giving Instructions, page 186

124    Planning Meals, page 199

125    Preparing for a Stressful Conversation, page 200

127    Problem-Solving a Disagreement, page 202

129    Responding to Others' Feelings, page 204

134    Self-Reporting Own Behaviors, page 209

140    Using Appropriate Language, page 215

143    Using Spontaneous Problem-Solving, page 218

150    Being an Appropriate Role Model, page 225

158    Expressing Empathy and Understanding for Others, page 233

165    Maintaining Relationships, page 240

168    Managing Stress, page 243

170    Recognizing Moods of Others, page 245

172    Resolving Conflicts, page 247

180    Using Leisure Time, page 255

# Classroom behavior and academic performance

| Skill No. | Skill Name, Location |
|---|---|
| 1 | Following Instructions, page 63 |
| 2 | Accepting "No" for an Answer, page 65 |
| 3 | Talking with Others, page 67 |
| 5 | Accepting Criticism or a Consequence, page 71 |
| 6 | Disagreeing Appropriately, page 73 |
| 8 | Showing Sensitivity to Others, page 79 |
| 11 | Accepting Consequences, page 83 |
| 12 | Accepting Decisions of Authority, page 84 |
| 15 | Asking for Help, page 88 |
| 16 | Asking Questions, page 89 |
| 17 | Being on Time (Promptness), page 90 |
| 21 | Completing Homework, page 94 |
| 22 | Completing Tasks, page 95 |
| 24 | Contributing to Discussions (Joining in a Conversation), page 97 |
| 26 | Doing Good Quality Work, page 99 |

27    Following Rules, page 100

28    Following Written Instructions, page 101

30    Getting the Teacher's Attention, page 103

33    Ignoring Distractions by Others, page 106

37    Listening to Others, page 110

39    Maintaining an Appropriate Appearance, page 112

41    Making an Apology, page 114

47    Participating in Activities, page 120

50    Reporting Other Youths' Behavior (or Peer Reporting), page 123

51    Resisting Peer Pressure, page 124

54    Seeking Positive Attention, page 127

55    Showing Appreciation, page 128

57    Staying on Task, page 130

59    Using an Appropriate Voice Tone, page 132

63    Volunteering, page 136

64    Waiting Your Turn, page 137

66    Accepting Help or Assistance, page 139

72    Being Prepared for Class, page 145

79    Complying with School Dress Code, page 152

81    Concentrating on a Subject or Task, page 154

82    Contributing to Group Activities, page 155

88    Cooperating with Others, page 161

93    Dealing with an Accusation, page 166

103    Delaying Gratification, page 177

104    Displaying Effort, page 178

105    Displaying Sportsmanship, page 179

109    Expressing Pride in Accomplishments, page 183

110    Following Safety Rules, page 184

115    Keeping Property in Its Place, page 190

120    Managing Time, page 195

123    Persevering on Tasks and Projects, page 198

131    Responding to Teasing, page 206

133    Self-Correcting Own Behavior, page 208

136    Sharing Attention with Others, page 211

140    Using Appropriate Language, page 215

144    Using Study Skills, page 219

153    Being Patient, page 228

160    Formulating Strategies, page 235

# Interpersonal conflict and disagreement

**Skill No.**    **Skill Name, Location**

2    Accepting "No" for an Answer, page 65

3    Talking with Others, page 67

5    Accepting Criticism or a Consequence, page 71

6    Disagreeing Appropriately, page 73

7   Showing Respect, page 75

9   Accepting Apologies from Others, page 81

10   Accepting Compliments, page 82

14   Asking for Clarification, page 87

19   Choosing Appropriate Words to Say, page 92

23   Complying with Reasonable Requests, page 96

25   Correcting Another Person (or Giving Criticism), page 98

29   Getting Another Person's Attention, page 102

31   Giving Compliments, page 104

32   Greeting Others, page 105

33   Ignoring Distractions by Others, page 106

35   Interrupting Appropriately, page 108

37   Listening to Others, page 110

41   Making an Apology, page 114

45   Making Positive Statements about Others, page 118

51   Resisting Peer Pressure, page 124

53   Saying "No" Assertively, page 126

59   Using an Appropriate Voice Tone, page 132

60   Using Anger Control Strategies, page 133

65   Accepting Defeat or Loss, page 138

67   Accepting Winning Appropriately, page 140

70   Analyzing Social Situations, page 143

78   Communicating Honestly, page 151

84   Controlling Emotions, page 157

89   Coping with Anger and Aggression from Others, page 162

91   Coping with Conflict, page 164

93   Dealing with an Accusation, page 166

102   Dealing with Rejection, page 176

105   Displaying Sportsmanship, page 179

107   Expressing Feelings Appropriately, page 181

113   Giving Rationales, page 187

121   Negotiating with Others, page 196

125   Preparing for a Stressful Conversation, page 200

126   Preventing Trouble with Others, page 201

127   Problem-Solving a Disagreement, page 202

128   Responding to Complaints, page 203

129   Responding to Others' Feelings, page 204

141   Using Relaxation Strategies, page 216

142   Using Self-Talk or Self-Instruction, page 217

143   Using Spontaneous Problem-Solving, page 218

152   Being Assertive, page 227

157   Displaying Appropriate Control, page 232

158   Expressing Empathy and Understanding for Others, page 233

166    Making an Appropriate Complaint, page 241

170    Recognizing Moods of Others, page 245

172    Resolving Conflicts, page 247

178    Tolerating Differences, page 253

181    Using Self-Monitoring and Self-Reflection, page 256

# Friendship and dating

**Skill No.**        **Skill Name, Location**

2    Accepting "No" for an Answer, page 65

3    Talking with Others, page 67

4    Introducing Yourself, page 69

5    Accepting Criticism or a Consequence, page 71

6    Disagreeing Appropriately, page 73

7    Showing Respect, page 75

8    Showing Sensitivity to Others, page 79

9    Accepting Apologies from Others, page 81

10    Accepting Compliments, page 82

17    Being on Time (Promptness), page 90

18    Checking In (or Checking Back), page 91

19    Choosing Appropriate Words to Say, page 92

24    Contributing to Discussions (Joining in a Conversation), page 97

29    Getting Another Person's Attention, page 102

31    Giving Compliments, page 104

32    Greeting Others, page 105

36    Introducing Others, page 109

37    Listening to Others, page 110

39    Maintaining an Appropriate Appearance, page 112

40    Maintaining Personal Hygiene, page 113

42    Making a Request (Asking a Favor), page 115

43    Making a Telephone Call, page 116

45    Making Positive Statements about Others, page 118

50    Reporting Other Youths' Behavior (or Peer Reporting), page 123

53    Saying "No" Assertively, page 126

54    Seeking Positive Attention, page 127

55    Showing Appreciation, page 128

56    Showing Interest, page 129

62    Using Table Etiquette, page 135

69    Analyzing Skills Needed for Different Situations, page 142

77    Choosing Appropriate Friends, page 150

78    Communicating Honestly, page 151

80    Compromising with Others, page 153

82    Contributing to Group Activities, page 155

84    Controlling Emotions, page 157

85    Controlling Sexually Abusive Impulses toward Others, page 158

97    Dealing with Embarrassing Situations, page 171

101   Dealing with Group Pressure, page 175

102   Dealing with Rejection, page 176

106   Expressing Appropriate Affection, page 180

107   Expressing Feelings Appropriately, page 181

114   Interacting Appropriately with Members of the Opposite Sex, page 188

117   Making Decisions, page 192

118   Making New Friends, page 193

121   Negotiating with Others, page 196

130   Responding to Others' Humor, page 205

135   Setting Appropriate Boundaries, page 210

137   Sharing Personal Experiences, page 212

138   Suggesting an Activity, page 213

139   Using Appropriate Humor, page 214

152   Being Assertive, page 227

156   Differentiating Friends from Acquaintances, page 231

158   Expressing Empathy and Understanding for Others, page 233

164   Laughing at Oneself, page 239

167   Making Moral and Spiritual Decisions, page 242

178   Tolerating Differences, page 253

# Transition to independent living

**Skill No.**    **Skill Name, Location**

3     Talking with Others, page 67

4     Introducing Yourself, page 69

5     Accepting Criticism or a Consequence, page 71

6     Disagreeing Appropriately, page 73

13    Answering the Telephone, page 85

14    Asking for Clarification, page 87

15    Asking for Help, page 88

17    Being on Time (Promptness), page 90

22    Completing Tasks, page 95

26    Doing Good Quality Work, page 99

28    Following Written Instructions, page 101

32    Greeting Others, page 105

39    Maintaining an Appropriate Appearance, page 112

43    Making a Telephone Call, page 116

57    Staying on Task, page 130

58    Trying New Tasks, page 131

61    Using Structured Problem-Solving (SODAS), page 134

66    Accepting Help or Assistance, page 139

68    Advocating for Oneself, page 141

| | |
|---|---|
| 70 | Analyzing Social Situations, page 143 |
| 76 | Choosing Appropriate Clothing, page 149 |
| 90 | Coping with Change, page 163 |
| 95 | Dealing with Boredom, page 169 |
| 111 | Following Through on Agreements and Contracts, page 185 |
| 117 | Making Decisions, page 192 |
| 118 | Making New Friends, page 193 |
| 120 | Managing Time, page 195 |
| 122 | Organizing Tasks and Activities, page 197 |
| 124 | Planning Meals, page 199 |
| 145 | Working Independently, page 220 |
| 147 | Altering One's Environment, page 222 |
| 149 | Assessing Own Abilities, page 224 |
| 150 | Being an Appropriate Role Model, page 225 |
| 151 | Being a Consumer, page 226 |
| 154 | Budgeting and Managing Money, page 229 |
| 155 | Clarifying Values and Beliefs, page 230 |
| 160 | Formulating Strategies, page 235 |
| 161 | Gathering Information, page 236 |
| 163 | Interviewing for a Job, page 238 |
| 165 | Maintaining Relationships, page 240 |
| 166 | Making an Appropriate Complaint, page 241 |
| 167 | Making Moral and Spiritual Decisions, page 242 |
| 169 | Planning Ahead, page 244 |
| 171 | Resigning from a Job or Project, page 246 |
| 173 | Rewarding Yourself, page 248 |
| 174 | Seeking Professional Assistance, page 249 |
| 175 | Setting Goals, page 250 |
| 178 | Tolerating Differences, page 253 |
| 179 | Using Community Resources, page 254 |
| 180 | Using Leisure Time, page 255 |
| 182 | Using Strategies to Find a Job, page 257 |

# Interaction with supervisors and co-workers

| Skill No. | Skill Name, Location |
|---|---|
| 1 | Following Instructions, page 63 |
| 2 | Accepting "No" for an Answer, page 65 |
| 3 | Talking with Others, page 67 |
| 4 | Introducing Yourself, page 69 |
| 5 | Accepting Criticism or a Consequence, page 71 |
| 6 | Disagreeing Appropriately, page 73 |
| 10 | Accepting Compliments, page 82 |
| 11 | Accepting Consequences, page 83 |
| 12 | Accepting Decisions of Authority, page 84 |
| 14 | Asking for Clarification, page 87 |
| 15 | Asking for Help, page 88 |
| 18 | Checking In (or Checking Back), page 91 |
| 19 | Choosing Appropriate Words to Say, page 92 |

23   Complying with Reasonable Requests, page 96

24   Contributing to Discussions (Joining in a Conversation), page 97

25   Correcting Another Person (or Giving Criticism), page 98

31   Giving Compliments, page 104

42   Making a Request (Asking a Favor), page 115

49   Reporting Emergencies, page 122

55   Showing Appreciation, page 128

63   Volunteering, page 136

66   Accepting Help or Assistance, page 139

69   Analyzing Skills Needed for Different Situations, page 142

74   Caring for Others' Property, page 147

78   Communicating Honestly, page 151

80   Compromising with Others, page 153

88   Cooperating with Others, page 161

93   Dealing with an Accusation, page 166

98   Dealing with Failure, page 172

104  Displaying Effort, page 178

109  Expressing Pride in Accomplishments, page 183

121  Negotiating with Others, page 196

123  Persevering on Tasks and Projects, page 198

126  Preventing Trouble with Others, page 201

127  Problem-Solving a Disagreement, page 202

128  Responding to Complaints, page 203

132  Responding to Written Requests, page 207

134  Self-Reporting Own Behaviors, page 209

139  Using Appropriate Humor, page 214

145  Working Independently, page 220

148  Asking for Advice, page 223

156  Differentiating Friends from Acquaintances, page 231

158  Expressing Empathy and Understanding for Others, page 233

163  Interviewing for a Job, page 238

166  Making an Appropriate Complaint, page 241

170  Recognizing Moods of Others, page 245

171  Resigning from a Job or Project, page 246

172  Resolving Conflicts, page 247

178  Tolerating Differences, page 253

181  Using Self-Monitoring and Self-Reflection, page 256

182  Using Strategies to Find a Job, page 257

# References

Ang, R., & Hughes, J. (2001). Differential benefits of skills training with antisocial youth based on group composition: A meta-analytic investigation. **School Psychology Review, 31**(2), 164-185.

Arthur, M., Bochner, S., & Butterfield, N. (1999). Enhancing peer interactions within the context of play. **International Journal of Disability, Development, and Education, 46,** 367-381.

Azrin, N.H., Hake, D.G., Holz, W.C., & Hutchinson, R.R. (1965). Motivational aspects of escape from punishment. **Journal of Experimental Analysis of Behavior, 8,** 31-34.

Baer, D.M., & Wolf, M.M., (1970). The entry into natural communities of reinforcement. In R. Ulrich, T. Stachnik, and J. Mabry (Eds.), **Control of Human Behavior, Vol. 2** (pp. 319-324). Glenview, IL: Scott Foresman.

Bandura, A. (1989). Social cognitive theory. In V.R. Greenwich (Ed.), **Annals of child development** (pp.1-60). Greenwich, CT: Jai Press.

Berkowitz, L. (1983). Aversively stimulated aggression: Some parallels and difference in research with animals and humans. **American Psychologist, 38,** 1135-1144.

Cartledge, G., & Milburn, J.F. (Eds.) (1980). **Teaching social skills to children.** New York: Pergamon Press.

Cartledge, G., & Milburn, J.F. (1996). **Cultural diversity and social skills instruction: Understanding ethnic and gender differences.** Champaign, IL: Research Press.

Cruickshank, W.M., Morse, W.C., & Johns, J.S. (1980). **Learning disabilities: The struggle from adolescence toward adulthood.** Syracuse, NY: Syracuse University Press.

DeBaryshe, B.D., Patterson, G.R., & Capaldi, D.M. (1993). A performance model for academic achievement in early adolescent boys. **Developmental Psychology, 29,** 795-804.

Dishion, T.J. (1992, October). **An applied model of antisocial behavior.** Paper presented at a workshop for potential applicants for NIMH research grants to prevent youth violence, Bethesda, MD.

Dodge, K.A., Price, J.M., Bachorowski, J., & Newman, J.P. (1990). Hostile attribution: Biases in severely aggressive adolescents. **Journal of Abnormal Psychology, 99,** 385-392.

Elliott, D.S. (1992, October). **Correlates of youth violence, and designing evaluations of interventions.** Paper presented at workshop for potential applicants for NIMH research grants to prevent youth violence, Bethesda, MD.

Friedman, R.M., Quick, J., Mayo, J., & Palmer, J. (1983). Social skills training within a day treatment program for emotionally disturbed adolescents. In C. LeCroy (Ed.), **Social skills training for children and youth** (pp. 139-151). New York: Haworth Press.

Goldstein, A.P., Sprafkin, R.P., Gershaw, N.J., & Klein, P. (1980). The adolescent: Social skills training through structured learning. In G. Cartledge and J.F. Milburn (Eds.), **Teaching social skills to children** (pp. 249-279). New York: Pergamon Press.

Gresham, F.M. (1981). Social skills training with handicapped children: A review. **Review of Educational Research, 51,** 139-176.

Gresham, F. (1995). Best practices in social skills training. In A. Thomas and J. Grimes (Eds.), **Best practices in school psychology – III** (pp. 1021-1030). Washington, DC: The National Association of School Psychologists.

Gresham, F.M. (1998). Social skills training: Should we raze, remodel, or rebuild? **Behavioral Disorders, 24**(1), 19-25.

Gresham, F.M., Sugai, G., & Horner, R.H. (2001). Interpreting outcomes of social skills training for students with high-incidence disabilities. **Exceptional Children, 67,** 331-334.

Hansen, D.J., St. Lawrence, J.S., & Christoff, K.A. (1989). Group conversation-skills training with inpatient children and adolescents: Social validation, generalization, and maintenance. **Behavior Modification, 13,** 4-31.

Hartup, W.W., & Moore, S.G. (1990). Early peer relations: Developmental significance and prognostic implications. **Early Childhood Research Quarterly, 5**(1), 1-18.

Hazel, J.S., Schumaker, J.B., Sherman, J.A., & Sheldon-Wildgen, J.S. (1983). Social skills training with court-adjudicated youths. In C. LeCroy (Ed.), **Social skills training for children and youth** (pp. 117-137). New York: Haworth Press.

Howing, P.T., Wodarski, J.S., Kurtz, P.D., & Gaudin, J.M. (1990). The empirical base for the implementation of social skills training with maltreated children. **Social Work, 35,** 460-467.

Kamps, D., Royer, J., Dugan, E., Kravits, T., Gonzalez-Lopez, A., Garcia, J., Carnazzo, K., Morrison, L., & Kane, L.G. (2002). Peer training to facilitate social interaction for elementary students with autism and their peers. **Exceptional Children, 68,** 173-187.

Kazdin, A.E. (1985). **Treatment of antisocial behavior in children and adolescents.** Homewood, IL: The Dorsey Press.

Kinsey, S.J. (2000). **The relationship between prosocial behaviors and academic achievement in the primary multi-age classroom.** Unpublished doctoral dissertation, Loyola University, Chicago.

Ladd, G.W. (2000). The fourth R: Relationships as risks and resources following children's transition to school. **American Educational Research Association Division E Newsletter, 19**(1), 7, 9-11.

Ladd, G.W., & Profilet, S.M. (1996). The child behavior scale: A teacher-report measure of young children's aggressive, withdrawn, and prosocial behaviors. **Developmental Psychology, 32**(6), 1008-1024.

LeCroy, C.W. (1983). Social skills training with adolescents: A review. In C. LeCroy (Ed.), **Social skills training in children and youth** (pp. 117-137). New York: Haworth Press.

Mayer, G.R. (1995). Preventing antisocial behavior in the schools. **Journal of Applied Behavior Analysis, 28,** 467-478.

Mayer, G.R. (2001). Antisocial behavior: Its causes and prevention within our schools. **Education and Treatment of Children, 24**(4), 414-429.

McClellan, D.E., & Kinsey, S. (1999). Children's social behavior in relation to participation in mixed-age or same-age classrooms. **Early Childhood Research & Practice** [On-line], 1(1). Available: http://ecrp.uiuc.edu/v1n1/v1n1.html.

Moyer, J., & Dardig, J.C. (1978). Practical task analysis for special educators. **Teaching Exceptional Children, 3,** 16-18.

Oden, S. (1980). A child's social isolation: Origins, prevention, intervention. In G. Cartledge and J.F. Milburn (Eds.), **Teaching social skills to children** (pp. 179-202). New York: Pergamon Press.

Parker, J.G., & Asher, S.R. (1987). Peer relations and later personal adjustment: Are low-accepted children at risk? **Psychological Bulletin, 102**(3), 357-389.

Patterson, G.R. (1982). **Coercive family process.** Eugene, OR: Castalia.

Robinson, T.R., Smith, S.W., Miller, M.D., & Brownell, M.T. (1999). Cognitive behavior modification of hyperactivity/impulsivity and aggression: A meta-analysis of school-based studies. **Journal of Educational Psychology, 91,** 195-203.

Rogoff, B.M. (1990). **Apprenticeship in thinking: Cognitive development in social context.** New York: Oxford University Press.

Shivrattan, J.L. (1988). Social interactional training and incarcerated juvenile delinquents. **Canadian Journal of Criminology, 4,** 145-163.

Spence, S.H. (2003). Social skills training with children and young people: Theory, evidence, and practice. **Child and Adolescent Mental Health, 8**(2), 84-96.

Spence, S.H., & Donovan, C. (1998). Interpersonal problems. In P. Graham (Ed.), **Cognitive-behaviour therapy for children and families** (pp. 217-245). Cambridge: Cambridge University Press.

Sterba, M., & Dowd, T. (1998). **Treating youth with DSM-IV disorders: The role of social skill instruction.** Boys Town Press: Boys Town, NE.

Stokes, T.F., & Baer, D.M. (1977). An implicit technology of generalization. **Journal of Applied Behavior Analysis, 10,** 349-367.

Sulzer-Azaroff, B., & Mayer, G.R. (1986). **Achieving educational excellence using behavioral strategies.** New York: Holt, Rinehart and Winston.

Trower, P., Bryant, B., & Argyle, M. (1978). **Social skills and mental health.** Pittsburgh: University of Pittsburgh Press.

Walker, H.M., Ramsey, E., & Gresham, F.M. (2004). **Antisocial behavior in school: Evidence-based practices.** Belmont, CA: Thomson/Wadsworth.

Wolf, M.M. (1978) Social validity: The case for subjective measurement or how applied behavior analysis is finding its heart. **Journal of Applied Behavioral Analysis, 11,** 203-214.

# Bibliography

Ang, R.P., & Hughes, J.N. (2001). Differential benefits of skills training with antisocial youth based on group composition: A meta-analytic investigation. **School Psychology Review, 31**(2), 164-185.

Antshel, K.M., & Remer, R. (2003). Social skills training in children with attention deficit hyperactivity disorder: A randomized-controlled clinical trail. **Journal of Clinical Child and Adolescent Psychology, 32**(1), 153-165.

Arbuthnot, J., & Gordon, D.A. (1986). Behavioral and cognitive effects of a moral reasoning development intervention for high-risk behavior-disordered adolescents. **Journal of Consulting and Clinical Psychology, 54**(2), 208-216.

Blake, C., Wang, W., Cartledge, G., & Gardner, R. (2000). Middle-school students with serious emotional disturbances serve as social skills trainers and reinforcers for peers with SED. **Behavioral Disorders, 25**(4), 280-298.

Cartledge, G., & Adedapo, V. (1998). Teacher and parent assessments of the social competence of inner-city children: Issues of gender within race. **Journal of Negro Education, 1**(2), 115-126.

Cartledge, G., & Loe, S.A. (2001). Cultural diversity and social skill instruction. **Exceptionality, 9**(1-2), 33-46.

Doughty, J.E. (1997, June). **The effect of a social skills curriculum on student performance.** ED412260. Paper presented at the Annual Research Colloquium (3rd), Carrollton, GA.

Feng, H., & Cartledge, G. (1996). Social skill assessment of inner city Asian, African, and European American students. **School Psychology Review, 25**(2), 228-239.

Ferguson, S.A. (1993). Facilitating multicultural competence. **Journal of Emotional and Behavioral Problems, 2**(4), 28-30.

Gibbs, J.C., Potter, G.B., Goldstein, A.P., & Brendtro, L. (1996). From harassment to helping with antisocial youth: The EQUIP program. **Reclaiming Children and Youth: Journal of Emotional and Behavioral Problems, 5**(1), 40-46.

Greco, L.A., & Morris, T.L. (2001). Treating childhood shyness and related behavior: Empirically evaluated approaches to promote positive social interactions. **Clinical Child and Family Psychology Review, 4**(4), 299-318.

Gresham, F.M. (1997). Social competence and students with behavior disorders: Where we've been, where we are, and where we should go. **Education and Treatment of Children, 20**(3), 233-249.

Gresham, F.M. (1998). Social skills training: Should we raze, remodel, or rebuild? **Behavioral Disorders, 24**(1), 19-25.

Gresham, F.M., Noell, G.H., & Elliott, S.N. (1996). Teachers as judges of social competence: A conditional probability analysis. **School Psychology Review, 25**(1), 108-117.

Gresham, F.M., Sugai, G., & Horner, R.H. (2001). Interpreting outcomes of social skills training for students with high-incidence disabilities. **Exceptional Children, 67**(3), 331-344.

Goldstein, A.P., & McGinnis, E. (1997). **Skillstreaming the adolescent: New strategies and perspectives for teaching prosocial skills.** Champaign, IL: Research Press.

Hansen, D.J., Nangle, D.W., & Meyer, K.A. (1998). Enhancing the effectiveness of social skills inteventions with adolescents. **Education and Treatment of Children, 21**(4), 489-513.

Hensley, M., Dillon, J.C., Pratt, D., Ford, J., & Burke, R. (2005). **Tools for teaching social skills in school: Lesson plans, activities, and blended teaching techniques to help your students succeed.** Boys Town, NE: Boys Town Press.

Hollin, C.R., & Trower, P. (1986). **Handbook of social skills training: Applications across the life span, Vol. 1.** Oxford, England: Pergamon Press.

Hollin, C.R., & Trower, P. (1986). **Handbook of social skills training: Applications across the life span, Vol. 2.** Oxford, England: Pergamon Press.

Liberman, R.P., & Martin, T. (2002). **Social skills training.** Peoria, IL: Behavioral Health Recovery Management Project.

Losel, F., & Beelmann, A. (2003). Effects of child skills training in preventing antisocial behavior: A systematic review of randomized evaluations. **The ANNALS of the American Academy of Political and Social Science, 587**(1), 84-109.

Mayer, G.R. (2001). Antisocial behavior: Its causes and prevention within our schools. **Education and Treatment of Children, 24**(4), 414-429.

Mellard, D., & Hazel, J.S. (1992). Social competencies as a pathway to successful life transitions. **Learning Disability Quarterly, 15,** 251-271.

Rivera, B.D., & Rogers-Atkinson, D. (1997). Culturally sensitive interventions: Social skills training with children and parents from culturally and linguistically diverse backgrounds. **Intervention in School and Clinic, 33**(2), 75-80.

Russman, S.B. (1997). **Social skills training for children and adolescents with a traumatic brain injury.** University of Utah, Dept. of Educational Psychology (Doctoral Dissertation).

Schumaker, J.B. (1992). Social performance of individuals with learning disabilities: Through the looking glass of KU-IRLD research. **School Psychology Review, 21**(3), 387-399.

Spence, S.H. (2003). Social skills training with children and young people: Theory, evidence, and practice. **Child and Adolescent Mental Health, 8**(2), 84-96.

Spence, S.H., Donovan, C., & Brechman-Toussaint, M. (2000). The treatment of childhood social phobia: The effectiveness of a social skills training-based, cognitive-behavioral intervention, with and without parental involvement. **Journal of Child Psychiatry, 41**(6), 713-726.

Taylor, G. (1993). **The relationship between social skills development, academic achievement and interpersonal relations of African-American males.** ERIC Document Reproduction Service (EDRS), ED390819.

Volz, J.R., Snyder, T., and Sterba, M. (2009). **Teaching social skills to youth with mental health disorders.** Boys Town Press: Boys Town, NE.

Webster-Stratton, C., Reid, J., & Hammond, M. (2001). Social skills and problem-solving training for children with early-onset conduct problems: Who benefits? **Journal of Child Psychology and Psychiatry, 42**(7), 941-952.

Weissberg, R.P., & Caplan, M. (1998). **Promoting social competence and preventing antisocial behavior in young urban adolescents.** Laboratory for Student Success: Temple University Center for Research in Human Development and Education, Pub. No. 22, pp. 1-22.

Zimmerman, D.P. (2002). Research and practice in social- and life-skills training. **Residential Treatment for Children & Youth, 20**(2), 51-75.

# Index

## A

Accepting Apologies from Others, 56, 81
Accepting Compliments, 56, 82
Accepting Consequences, 15, 25, 48, 56, 62, 71-72, 83
Accepting Criticism, 15, 22, 25, 33, 38, 56, 62, 71-72, 142, 200
Accepting Decisions of Authority, 15, 56, 84
Accepting Defeat or Loss, 57, 138
Accepting Help or Assistance, 57, 139
Accepting "No" for an Answer, 2, 11, 13, 15, 22, 25-26, 42-43, 48, 56, 61, 65-66, 115, 146
Accepting Self, 58, 221
Accepting Winning Appropriately, 57, 140
acknowledging instructions, 13-14, 20-21, 24, 27-29, 96
Advocating for Oneself, 57, 141
aggression, 8, 11-12, 17, 26, 34, 48-49, 83, 162-164
Altering One's Environment, 58, 222
Analyzing Skills Needed for Different Situations, 57, 142
Analyzing Social Situations, 57, 143
Analyzing Tasks to be Completed, 57, 144
Answering the Telephone, 56, 85-86
antecedent events, 11-12, 19, 23, 49
    components of, 12-13
Asking for Advice, 58, 223
Asking for Clarification, 56, 87
Asking for Help, 56, 88, 131
Asking Questions, 56, 89
Assessing Own Abilities, 58, 224

## B

behavior
    analysis, 4, 11
        model, 13
    antisocial, 48, 53
    assessment, 8, 11, 14
    definition of, 13
    describing, 19, 20-21, 23-24, 26-29
    expectations, 34, 44
    external problem, 8
    functional relationships of, 11-13
    improvements in, 22, 222
    internal problem, 8
    modeling, 7, 17, 19, 28, 39-40
        negative, 7
    monitoring, 44, 56
    negative, 2-4, 8-9, 11, 14, 19, 26, 45, 48-49, 54
        correcting, 17, 30
        decreasing, 12,
        preventing, 17
        rewarding, 17
    patterns, self-defeating, 4, 8
    positive, 45
        increasing, 12
        punishing, 17
        reinforcing, 12, 17, 21, 25-26, 30, 34, 45, 54
    replacing, 3, 4, 8
    sequencing, 13-14
    sexual, 49, 57, 158, 225
    shaping, 2-3, 8-9, 12, 54
    social, 7, 11-15
    specifying, 17-18
behavioral principles, 3
"behavior trap," 34
Being a Consumer, 58, 226
Being an Appropriate Role Model, 58, 225
Being Assertive, 58, 227
Being Honest, 14
Being on Time (Promptness), 56, 90
Being Patient, 58, 228
Being Prepared for Class, 57, 145

Borrowing from Others, 57, 146

Boys Town

    Assessment and Short-Term Residential
        Program, 3

    Ecological Family-Based Services
        Program, 3, 4

    Ecological Treatment Foster Care Program,
        3, 4, 9

    Long-Term Residential Program, 2-3, 4

    Social Skills Curriculum, 4, 14, 49

    Teaching Model, 3-4, 17, 45

Budgeting and Managing Money, 58, 229

# C

caring, 1-2, 5

Caring for Others' Property, 15, 57, 147

Caring for Own Belongings, 57, 148

CHARACTER COUNTS! Coalition, 1-2

Checking In (or Checking Back), 56, 91

child-care technology, 2, 3

Choosing Appropriate Clothing, 57, 149

Choosing Appropriate Friends, 57, 150

Choosing Appropriate Words to Say, 56, 92

citizenship, 1, 5

Clarifying Values and Beliefs, 58, 230

Closing a Conversation, 56, 93

cognitive mediators, 34

Communicating Honestly, 15, 57, 151

communication

    clear, 7, 12-14, 18, 34, 73

    problems with, 17

    unclear, 12

compassion, 2, 3

Completing Homework, 56, 94

Completing Tasks, 56, 95

Complying with Reasonable Requests, 56, 96

Complying with School Dress Code, 57, 152

Compromising with Others, 15, 28-29, 57, 153

Concentrating on a Subject or Task, 57, 154

consequent events/consequences, 12-13, 26, 29,
    47, 192, 252

    identifying, 12

    natural/logical, 35, 159, 218

    negative, 26-29, 34-35, 44, 49, 51

    positive, 20-21, 23, 24, 27, 29, 40, 43-44

    punishing, 12-13

    reinforcing, 12-13

Contributing to Discussions (Joining in a
    Conversation), 56, 97

Contributing to Group Activities, 57, 155

Controlling Eating Habits, 57, 156

Controlling Emotions, 15, 57, 157

Controlling Sexually Abusive Impulses toward
    Others, 57, 158

Controlling the Impulse to Lie, 57, 159

Controlling the Impulse to Steal, 15, 57, 160

Cooperating with Others, 57, 161

Coping with Anger and Aggression from
    Others, 15, 57, 162

Coping with Change, 57, 163

Coping with Conflict, 57, 164

Coping with Sad Feelings (or Depression), 57, 165

Correcting Another Person (or Giving
    Criticism), 56, 98, 176

correction statements, 27, 29

culture, 49, 80

# D

Dealing with Accusations, 15, 57, 166-167

Dealing with Being Left Out, 57, 168

Dealing with Boredom, 5, 167

Dealing with Contradictory Messages, 57, 170

Dealing with Embarrassing Situations, 57, 171

Dealing with Failure, 57, 172

Dealing with Fear, 57, 173

Dealing with Frustration, 15, 57, 174

Dealing with Group Pressure, 57, 175

Dealing with Rejection, 57, 176

Delaying Gratification, 57, 177

delinquency, 2, 8, 38, 169, 225

depression, 8, 53, 163, 165

Differentiating Friends from Acquaintances, 58,
    231

Disagreeing Appropriately, 2, 15, 25, 56, 62,
    73-74, 170, 176, 200, 228

Displaying Appropriate Control, 58, 232

Displaying Effort, 57, 178

Displaying Sportsmanship, 57, 179

Doing Good Quality Work, 56, 99

# E

empathy, 27-29, 38, 203-204, 233
empowerment, 3, 29, 54
Expressing Appropriate Affection, 57, 180
Expressing Concern and Understanding for
    Others, 15
Expressing Empathy and Understanding for
    Others, 58, 233
Expressing Feelings Appropriately, 15, 57, 181
Expressing Grief, 58, 234
Expressing Optimism, 57, 182
Expressing Pride in Accomplishments, 57, 183

# F

"fair fighting," 44-45
fairness, 1, 5
Family Meeting, 45
feedback, 17, 23, 24, 27, 28, 29, 44, 131, 155
Flanagan, Father Edward, 2
Following Instructions, 1-2, 11, 13-15, 22-25,
    28, 33, 35, 38, 48, 56, 61, 63-64, 142, 170
Following Rules, 15, 17, 56, 100
Following Safety Rules, 58, 184
Following Through on Agreements and
    Contracts, 58, 185
Following Written Instructions, 101
Formulating Strategies, 58, 235

# G

Gathering Information, 58, 236
generalization, 2, 4, 13-14, 18, 23, 38, 54
    assignments, 40, 43
    promoting, 17, 30, 34-35, 39
    training, 33-45
Getting Along with Others, 22
Getting Another Person's Attention, 102
Getting the Teacher's Attention, 15, 34, 56, 103
Giving Compliments, 56, 104
Giving Instructions, 58, 186
Giving Rationales, 58, 186, 187, 196, 213
Golden Rule, 5
Greeting Others, 56, 105, 142

# I

Identifying Own Feelings, 58, 237
Ignoring Distractions by Others, 56, 106
Initiating a Conversation, 56, 107
Interacting Appropriately with the Opposite
    Sex, 15, 58, 188-190
internalization, 2, 18, 54
Interrupting Appropriately, 15, 56, 108
interventions, 4, 34, 48
    determining, 8, 44
    primary, 9
    restrictive, 9
    secondary, 9
    skill-based, 14, 38-39
    tertiary, 9
Interviewing for a Job, 58, 238
Introducing Others, 56, 109
Introducing Yourself, 56, 61, 69-70

# J

Joseph & Edna Josephson Institute of Ethics, 1

# K

Keeping Property in Its Place, 15, 58, 190

# L

Laughing at Oneself, 58, 239
Lending to Others, 58, 191, 191
Listening to Others, 15, 56, 110

# M

Maintaining a Conversation, 56, 111
Maintaining an Appropriate Appearance, 56,
    112
Maintaining Personal Hygiene, 56, 113
Maintaining Relationships, 58, 240
Making a Request (Asking a Favor), 25, 56,
    115
Making a Telephone Call, 56, 116
Making an Apology, 15, 56, 114
Making an Appropriate Complaint, 58, 241
Making Decisions, 58, 192

Making Moral and Spiritual Decisions, 58, 242
Making New Friends, 15, 58, 193
Making Positive Self-Statements, 56, 117
Making Positive Statements about Others, 15, 57, 118
Making Restitution (Compensation), 15, 58, 194
Managing Stress, 58, 243
Managing Time, 58, 195
mental health disorders, 8, 48
motivation systems, 35

# N

Negotiating with Others, 15, 58, 196

# O

Offering Assistance or Help, 57, 119
Organizing Tasks and Activities, 58, 197

# P

Participating in Activities, 57, 120
peer
    acceptance, 12, 14
    conflicts, 44-45
    negative, 2, 14, 39
    positive, 2
    reporting, 57, 123, 166, 184, 205, 206, 209
Persevering on Tasks and Projects, 58, 198
Planning Ahead, 58, 244
Planning Meals, 58, 199
popularity, 14
practice, 7, 8, 17, 23-29, 33
praise, 25-29, 35, 44, 98, 155, 157
    Effective, 19-22, 23, 30, 49
        steps of, 20-21
        when to use, 21-22
    general, 2
Preparing for a Stressful Conversation, 58, 200
Preventing Trouble with Others, 58, 201
Problem-Solving a Disagreement, 15, 58, 202
program departure, 49
prompts, 24-25, 40
    preventive, 25

# R

rationales, 20, 21, 23, 24, 27, 28, 29, 30, 34, 48, 56, 63, 64, 65-66, 67-68, 69-80, 141, 186-187, 196, 213
Recognizing Moods of Others, 58, 246
Refraining from Possessing Contraband or Drugs, 57, 121
reinforcement, 34, 44
    appropriate, 8
    contingencies, 30
    external, 3
    inconsistent, 7, 17
Reporting Emergencies, 57, 122
Reporting Other Youths' Behavior (or Peer Reporting), 57, 123, 166, 184, 205, 206, 209
Resigning from a Job or Project, 58, 246
Resisting Peer Pressure, 14, 38, 57, 124
Resolving Conflicts, 58, 247
Responding to Complaints, 58, 203
Responding to Others' Feelings, 58, 204
Responding to Others' Humor, 58, 205
Responding to Teasing, 58, 206
Responding to Written Requests, 58, 207
responsibility, 1, 5, 30, 44, 181
Rewarding Yourself, 58, 248
role-playing, 17, 24, 26, 33, 40, 42-43, 44

# S

Saying Good-Bye to Guests, 57, 125
Saying "No" Assertively, 57, 124, 126, 175
Seeking Positive Attention, 15, 57, 127
Seeking Professional Assistance, 58, 249
self-confidence, 19, 28, 30
self-control, 7, 8, 9
    loss of, 26
Self-Correcting Own Behavior, 58, 208
self-esteem, 8, 222
self-government, 45
    promoting, 3
Self-Reporting Own Behaviors, 58, 160, 166, 209
Setting Appropriate Boundaries, 58, 210

Setting Goals, 58, 250
Sharing Attention with Others, 58, 211
Sharing Personal Experiences, 58, 212
Showing Appreciation, 57, 128
Showing Interest, 57, 129
Showing Respect, 15, 56, 62, 75-77
Showing Sensitivity to Others, 15, 56, 62,
    79-80
sincerity, 19, 23, 73, 139, 214
Six Pillars of Character, 1-2, 5
skills
    academic, 4, 6, 8
    advanced, 57-58, 138-220
    alternate, 12
    basic, 55, 56, 61-80
    choosing, 8, 12-13, 14
    complex, 55, 58-59, 221-257
    deficits, 11-12, 22-23, 25, 49
    definition of, 13
    emotional management, 4, 6, 8, 9
    ethical/moral, 4, 6
    for conduct-disordered youth, 14, 15
    identifying, 17, 23-24
    independent-living, 4, 6
    intermediate, 56-57, 81-137
    learning new, 22-23
    problem-solving, 4, 7, 9, 17, 34
        interpersonal, 8
    social
        assigning, 48-49
        components of, 13-14, 17-18
        defining, 1, 2, 6, 7, 40
        generalization of, 33-45
        modeling, 40, 41, 42
        targeting, 9, 13, 51
        teaching/training, 1, 3, 4, 7, 7-8, 12, 14,
            17, 30, 48
            benefits of, 8-9
            Boys Town's approach, 2-3
            goals of, 2, 11
            group, 4, 9, 30, 37-45, 55
                advantages of, 37-39
                format of, 39-44
                productive, 44-45

        individual, 4, 9, 17-31
        opportunities for, 15-19
        philosophy of, 8
        short-term benefits of, 2
        two-dimensional model of, 7-8
    treatment-oriented, 25
social
    acquisition deficits, 7, 8
    competence, 7-8, 13
        developing, 8
        minimal, 47
    fluency deficits, 7, 8, 12, 14, 22-23, 47
    information, 8
    integration, 14
    performance deficits, 7, 8
    skills
        acquisition, 8
        assigning, 48-49
        components of, 13-14, 17-18
        defining, 1, 2, 6, 7, 40
        generalization of, 33-45
        modeling, 40, 41, 42
        targeting, 9, 13, 51
        teaching/training, 1, 3, 4, 7, 7-8, 12, 14,
            17, 30, 48
            benefits of, 8-9
            Boys Town's approach, 2-3
            goals of, 2, 11
            group, 4, 9, 30, 37-45, 55
                advantages of, 37-39
                format of, 39-44
                productive, 44-45
            individual, 4, 9, 18
            opportunities for, 15-19
            philosophy of, 8
            short-term benefits of, 2
            two-dimensional model of, 7-8
sociometric measures, 14
spirituality, 3, 49
Staying on Task, 57, 130
Stopping Negative or Harmful Thoughts, 58,
    251
Suggesting an Activity, 58, 213

# T

Taking Risks Appropriately, 58, 252
Talking with Others, 33, 34, 56, 61, 67-68
tantrums, 11, 12
task analysis, 4, 13-14
    guidelines for, 14
Teaching,
    Corrective, 19, 26-30, 44, 49
        example, 28-29
        Interaction, 29
        steps of, 26-28
    Proactive, 19, 22-26, 30, 49
        steps of, 23-25
        when to use, 25-26
Tolerating Differences, 58, 253
*Tools for Teaching Social Skills in School*, 56
"trapping," 33-34
*Treating Youth with DSM-IV Disrders:*
    *The Role of Social Skill Instruction*, 53
treatment plan, 47-54
    additional assistance in, 53-54
    developing, 49-53
    follow-up, 52-53
    goals, 51-52
    individual, 45, 47, 49-53
    maintenance, 53
    monitoring, 52
    process, 50-53
    revising, 49, 52-53
    teams, 55
trustworthiness, 1, 5, 18
Trying New Tasks, 57, 131

# U

Using an Appropriate Voice Tone, 57, 132
Using Anger Control Strategies, 4, 15, 57, 133
Using Appropriate Humor, 58, 214
Using Appropriate Language, 58, 215
Using Community Resources, 59, 254
Using Leisure Time, 59, 255
Using Relaxation Strategies, 58, 216
Using Self-Monitoring and Self-Reflection,
    59, 256

Using Self-Talk or Self-Instruction, 58, 217
Using Spontaneous Problem-Solving, 58, 200,
    218
Using Strategies to Find a Job, 59, 257
Using Structured Problem-Solving (SODAS),
    57, 134
Using Study Skills, 58, 219
Using Table Etiquette, 57, 135

# V

Volunteering, 57, 136

# W

Waiting Your Turn, 15, 57, 137
Working Independently, 58, 220

# Book Offers Social Skill Lesson Plans for Teachers

*Dealing with disruptive behaviors* in the classroom can reduce the time a teacher has available for academic teaching. You can help prevent problem behaviors by teaching social skills to students. When children practice and learn how to behave in the classroom, they contribute to creating an environment that's calm, quiet, and conducive to successful learning.

## *This book provides teachers with:*

- Lesson plans for teaching 28 different social skills with activities that can be adapted for students in grades K-12. The plans include suggestions for discussion, activities, journaling, role-play, and reading.

- Reproducible skill pages that you can hand out or post in the classroom as reminders to students, and coupons you can use to reward good behavior.

- Techniques and examples for "blending" the teaching of social skills into academic lessons in reading, writing, math, and social studies.

- Ideas for using bulletin board displays to motivate and monitor behavior.

- Strategies for increasing parent support.

Available from Bookstores or from the Boys Town Press
1-800-282-6657 • boystownpress.org

*Tools for Teaching
Social Skills in School*
ISBN: 978-1-889322-64-3

The authors have a combined 40 years of teaching experience in K-12 classrooms, and train teachers, administrators, and other school staff across the United States in the Boys Town Education Model. The Model emphasizes building relationships with students, teaching social skills, and reinforcement of positive behavior.

The Boys Town Press offers many books, videos, and CDs useful to teachers, counselors, other youth-serving professionals, and parents.

For a free catalog:
Call 1-800-282-6657
Visit BoysTownPress.org

# More Social Skill Lesson Plans for the Classroom

Teaching children social skills gives them more behavioral choices, choices that are healthier for them, for you, for your classroom. When students learn the skills in this workbook, they help create a productive, collaborative, and cooperative learning environment.

In this book, 35 new lesson plans with activities will help you introduce to your students a range of social skills, from the basic (following instructions and listening to others) to the complex (advocating for yourself and setting long-term goals).

Lessons are written in an easy-to-follow format with talking points to help you define and explain a skill and guide students through an activity. At the end of each lesson is a *Think Sheet* for students with questions about how to use a skill in different settings and situations. Role-play scenarios are provided so students can practice each skill's behavioral steps. Additional classroom activities blend the teaching of social skills into academic lessons in math/science, language arts, social science, and physical education.

An ideal companion to *Tools for Teaching Social Skills in School,* this workbook features a CD-ROM with reproducible worksheets and skill posters (to hang in classrooms and common areas)! Some of the new social skills included are: expressing empathy, going to an assembly, accepting defeat or loss, using anger control strategies, responding to inappropriate talk/touch, completing homework, being prepared for class, and resisting negative peer pressure.

*More Tools for Teaching Social Skills in School*
Midge Odermann Mougey, Ed.D., et.al.
ISBN: 978-1-934490-04-4

Available from Bookstores or from the Boys Town Press
1-800-282-6657 • BoysTownPress.org

# Teaching Social Skills to Youth CD-ROM

This is a cross platform CD-ROM that will work on both Windows and Mac platforms.

## REQUIREMENTS

Display Settings: 800x600 or greater, 24 bit Color

Windows: Windows 2000, Windows XP, Windows 98 (Performance is decreased on older Windows 98 systems.)

MAC: Mac OS Classic (9.x) and Mac OS 10.x

This program requires you to download the appropriate version of Adobe Acrobat Reader. Visit Adobe's website at http://www.adobe.com/ to obtain the free reader.

## TO START

On Windows Systems: No installation is required. This program runs from the CD-ROM. Insert the CD-ROM. On Windows systems with the "Autorun" feature turned on, the program will launch automatically. If this does not occur, access your CD-ROM drive and double click on the icon labeled "Start."

Mac Systems: No installation is required. This program runs from the CD-ROM. Insert the CD-ROM and double click on "CD-ROM" icon. Select a folder that represents your Operating System ("MacClassic" or "MacOSX"). Then double click on the icon labeled "Start."

## NOTES

If you wish to bypass this program, you can access the PDF files directly by going to "D:\SKILLS" on the CD-ROM.